For Shannon

Acknowledgments

Special thanks to Nick Sedillos, Ellen Kleiner, Paul Enso Hillman & Ann Lowe for their help in preparing this book. And thanks to all my family & friends who appear in these pages (some of whose names have been changed). I love you all. Thanks also to Joe Romm at climateprogress.org for his tireless work & to James Hansen, Bill McKibben, Tim DeChristopher, Jim Corcoran, Josh Fox, Akilah & all environmental activists, as well as those who work for peace & justice. And finally, deepest gratitude to OR, APR, Ammachi & Garchen Rinpoche. May all beings be happy & free of suffering!

Contents

I permit to speak at every hazard
Nature without check with original energy

—Walt Whitman

Diverse sufferings are like the death of a child in
a dream. By apprehending illusory appearances as
real, one becomes weary. Therefore, when encoun-
tering disagreeable circumstances, viewing them as
illusory is the Bodhisattvas' practice.

—Ngulchu Thogme Zangpo

Chapter 1
Goodbye Florida

December 28, 2010

How much fuel does a 777 use per minute?

Answers.com: That will depend on the cruise altitude & Mach speed setting. Typical cruise will be around 13,000 pounds per hour; roughly 31 gallons per minute.

Result: more global warming. My plane trip will produce roughly the same CO_2 as driving it alone would. Air travel in the US consumes 1.4 million barrels of oil a day. I'm flying from Albuquerque to Tampa International Airport. I grew up in St. Petersburg, across the bay from there. That's where I lived from age 10 to 18. I've visited off & on for 48 years now from my home in New Mexico.

What has changed in half a century? Sea level has risen 4 inches for one thing & there are a lot more people living there.

The plane is full of oblivious polluters. My motivation is to somehow help beings but I'll kill some with this trip. I don't know who or where or when but the burning of fossil jet fuel will speed up climate & biosphere disruption just as any trip to the store in a car will. We're not intending to kill but one thing leads to another. I do some purification mantras. I wish we were using bio-fuel from algae or something. Kids on the plane. What kind of future are we creating for them?

Southwest Airlines magazine has a story on Florida waters. Ponce de Leon visited in 1513, seeking the legendary Fountain of Youth. But the fresh water aquifers will be flooded with salt as the sea level continues to rise. Greenland is melting fast. Totally melted it would add 17 feet to the sea level. And Antarctica is melting too. Millions of climate refugees with nowhere to go will leave the coasts & eventually the whole peninsula. Walt Whitman exclaimed: "Always Florida's green peninsula!" But he couldn't foresee how humans could alter the earth.

Where will people go?

Maybe hotels & motels will house the refugees. Maybe there will be tent cities & FEMA trailers.

Maybe there won't be gas for transportation. The destinations will already be struggling with their own stresses: droughts, floods, food shortages, infrastructure collapses. If there is a sudden rise in the seas, people & animals will die.

How gradual or sudden will it be? Climate scientists don't know. But when the methyl hydrates in the ocean begin melting—frozen methane releasing the greenhouse gas 20 times as potent as CO_2—a feedback loop will be underway that will accelerate the climate changes rapidly. 2010 CO_2 was 389.78 parts per million. James Hansen & others say that earth needs to get back below 350 ppm to be a decent place to live. That means we must get back to 1987 levels. But we are going up. When will it peak? At what overheated level?

I'm a Buddhist. I pray a lot to my teachers. Om Mani Padme Hung. May all beings be happy & free of suffering...

The corporate media love BAU (Business As Usual). *USA Today* has a nice graphic of the record cold hitting Florida now. It shows the North Atlantic Oscillation to be negative; the jet stream way south. But no view of the Arctic or mention of climate change. Weather is just an interesting page. BBC under orders to not mention climate change. (It's old news.) One has to search out climate science. I get mine from climateprogress.org.

The atmosphere from 35,000 feet: H_2O vapor, a GHG (greenhouse gas) is increasing with warmer temperatures. Another feedback loop. Pretty blanket of white cotton clouds. To be 73 degrees in St. Pete on Friday.

Clear now. We're flying over dark Gulf of Mexico. Oil rig lights dot the abyss.

Ignorance leads to using fossil fuels leads to suffering which is only beginning.

My sister & brother-in-law meet me at the airport. Warm greetings on a cold night. I notice that I'm not the only one aging. We drive through St. Pete & over the Skyway bridge to Terra Ceia Island. David builds a quick fire & goes to bed. Sue & I & Nicholas the kitten get warm. Nice hug from sister before bed.

December 29

Morning ngöndro, the foundational practices. Over the last 7 years I've done 100,000 refuge prayers, 100,000 bodhicitta prayers (the wish that all beings attain enlightenment), 200,000 purification mantras &

100,000 mandala offerings. Now I'm working on 1.3 million vajra guru mantras for guru yoga. Om ah hung vajra guru padme siddhi hung!

It's the coldest December in 115 years in Miami. It's the negative NAO. Frost in the yard.

After breakfast, 2 nice Jehovah's Witnesses come up the stairs to the house. I tell them I'm Buddhist, impatiently. But I relax when one says there are probably things we share. He's right. I check out the book I'm offered. Page 62, "spirit creatures." Oh, they mean angels & demons. As a Tibetan Buddhist, I can relate to that somewhat. But I don't want the book. Have a nice day!

I decide to interview my sister. Where does your water come from? She says it comes from the county. They used to have a well, with sulfur water. Maybe it comes from the Peace River now. What was the sea level rise the last 100 years? 6 inches, she guesses. Close: 7.8 inches. Do you have flood insurance? Yes, it's required by Terra Ceia. All houses in the area have to have their living quarters on the second floor. How long till your house is uninhabitable due to climate change? She answers: 200 years. If it was uninhabitable in your lifetime, where would you go? San Francisco...

For myself, living in Albuquerque, my guess is 20 years until the house is uninhabitable. Drought would be the problem, say the experts. Where would I go? Denver, to be close to OR, my US teacher? Mill Creek in Pennsylvania, the old, undeveloped family property? How can you plan in the midst of such uncertainty?

Sue reads 2 newspapers, Sierra Magazine from the Sierra Club; listens to NPR & watches NBC Nightly News. But still thinks it's going to be 200 years till the flood. It's just not sinking in that the future is coming closer all the time. Climate Progress says sea level rise (SLR) of 6 feet by 2100 is dead certain. That would be a foot in 15 years with BAU. An inch per year. CO_2 levels haven't been this high for 15 million years, when it was 5–10 degrees F. warmer & seas were 75-120 feet higher.

Brother Bob drives over from St. Pete for dinner. He brings the healthy pie & soy dream.

December 30

Sue & I go birding. We see a painted bunting! Blue head, red body, green wings for the male. The female is just greenish-yellow. Sexual selection is amazing. Back at the house with the Sibley's Bird Book, I see the bit about extinct species. Florida used to be home to the Dusky Seaside Sparrow. Habitat loss led to its extinction in 1980.

The Florida panther is also running out of habitat—100 of them left. I eat an orange from the tree. Warm day.

St. Petersburg Times, Dec. 30, 2010: "Record heat to cruel cold." The year in review reads: "This year's weather was unlike anything Tampa Bay has seen in the 120 years records have been kept." There's nothing on climate change specifically though. On the editorial page: "Keep Everglades on track." Millions of dollars wasted, in my opinion. Florida is going under.

December 31

I bike around the island with Sue as guide. Some houses are for sale or empty; some have only one floor.

We go over to neighbor's for New Year's Eve bonfire. Tom & I play songs under the royal palms with stars above. How it might have been at the birth of Jesus. Kids get excited by fireworks. 2011 begins...

January 1

An old book on my sister's shelf is "On Death & Dying."

According to Elisabeth Kubler-Ross, MD, the five stages of dying are:

1. Denial & Isolation
2. Anger
3. Bargaining
4. Depression
5. Acceptance

I'm trying to be at 5; but most media at 1. Most people at 1. I'm 66 years old; maybe that has something to do with it. Plus, awareness of impermanence & death is a necessary part of my daily meditations. Could these be the stages of climate change awareness too?

Sue & David have lived here for 19 years. There are 300 homes on the island. Attachment to home is very strong. There is a pride of place. There is the financial investment. There is familiarity & security. There is one's job.

Inertia: personal, social. How do you move 20 million people?

The new governor of Florida is billionaire, Rick Scott, Republican. He was CEO of Columbia/HCA, once the largest private for-profit health care company in the US. Rick was forced to resign after the company admitted to 14 felonies, eventually shelling out 2 billion dollars in the largest fraud settlement in US history. He says he will add 700,000 jobs in 7 years. Also, he will freeze regulations & drill for oil in an "environmentally friendly manner." Just when compassionate planning is needed for the disruptions of climate change & peak oil, Scott will cut social programs & subsidize corporations. Paul Krugman: "Banana republic, here we come."

Economic growth is good for humans but bad for the other species with which we share the earth. But ultimately, growth is bad for humans too.

Is Terra Ceia really an island? Not according to the map on an official sign. We see it after biking to Bishop Harbor. I guess nobody ever tried going around the "island." The state is trying to preserve the land from invasive species & the seagrass from boats. Manatee grass, Turtle grass & Shoal grass are getting shredded. Terra Ceia is Portuguese for "heavenly land." Nice oaks with Spanish moss.

Wisconsin (David's team) loses the Rose Bowl.

January 2

I show my sister the photos of APR disappearing. He's my root lama, now living in Chinese-occupied Tibet & not able to travel. (I haven't seen him in 3 years.) For security, I'll just call him APR, the R standing for Rinpoche, which means precious teacher. Not much comment from Sue. Now she's back into her 2 newspapers. How can someone disappear? Mind over matter? Or is it some trick of the camera?

I walk the perimeter of the property. A flock of white ibises. Where will they go when Greenland melts? Impermanence of life. Suffering.

Tampa Bay Bucs win their last game of the season.

I pack up & we head for the St. Pete Beach condos. The family has 2. I will stay the rest of my Florida visit in The Friendly Native. Bob brings his lovely daughter, Celia, out. I call my daughter, Shannon, in Taos & pass around the phone. She's happy: "Dad, let's all go to Florida for Spring break!" I say something like "we'll see," the all-purpose response from my parents. I'm writing in the notebook she gave me for

Christmas. It's home-made, bound with string. On the cover are musical clefs with the mantra Om mani padme hung as the notes of the melody. Maybe I'll write a book about this trip.

I walk out to the Gulf after dinner by myself. The acidifying ocean; waves of doom.

January 3

Paper: "Cars go green, but buyers like SUVs." Prius sales drop 1.7%. Normal low is 53 degrees; yesterday's low 62. Blanket of GHGs keeps the warmth in at night. Floods swamping Australia, an area equal to France plus Germany. Days of rain there.

TV: demand from China to raise gas prices in US to $3.75 by Spring. Maybe then the Prius, Leaf & Volt sales will pick up.

Royal terns on beach, innocent of altering the atmosphere, the ocean, the biosphere. Tide-line almost to the little dunes with their sea oats. Beach repair to the north. I am a temporary resident of Long Key. Where does my fresh water originate? Where does my electricity come from? Coal, I believe. How long till the condos are uninhabitable? By the end of Scott's first term? Second term? Need to see the graphs. With BAU, pretty darn soon...

Seashores, A Golden Guide: "The seas cover about 72% of the earth's surface—61% of the northern & 81% of the southern hemisphere." "The Gulf of Mexico has 1 or 2 foot tides; elsewhere they are 4 to 8 feet or more." Phytoplankton & zooplankton. 18,000 species of algae. 2,000 species of horny sponges. 15,000 species of bivalves. So many plants & animals, intricately evolved over eons. All threatened by dissolved CO_2 which makes carbonic acid. The acid has begun eating away at the lime shells of animals. So many beings caught in the wheel of birth & death.

And then there are the oil rigs & oil spills & the chemical dispersants. Oil is such a bad deal, from the well to the atmosphere. As is uranium.

NBC, 6:30: ice-storm in LA, floods in Australia. In Arkansas: 5,000 redwing blackbirds & 100,000 fish dead. Om Ami Dewa Hri. May they be born in the Pure Land of Amitabha.

January 4

Brother Bob drives us to Honeymoon Island State Park. Lots of ospreys there. Also a bald eagle nest. We eat by the peaceful waters at Pelican Point & I interview him. His water comes from the Ozona well fields in north Pinellas county. He was there once when he worked for the water department. I ask about electricity. From the Weedon Island coal plant he says & maybe some from the Crystal River nuclear plant. He guesses that sea level has risen 4 inches in the last century. Flood insurance not necessary at his house (where we all used to live). It's 24 feet above sea level. How long until his house is gone? 100 years he says. Where would he go if he had to leave? Waynesville, North Carolina or Mill Creek.

Bob's car gets 18 miles per gallon. He paid $28,000 for the slightly used Infiniti & some extra for more horsepower. Irascible brother next wants to find Booker Creek Park where Sierra Club meets. He has the big Florida map book. Cypress, developments, too many cars. I see that the book is 8 years out of date. The park has succumbed to housing. Habitat shrinking for wildlife; human population swelling. It's rush hour. "Life is brief" sings The Band on the CD Bob made for me.

I tell my brother that this could be my last trip to Florida. But I'll try to come back & help them evacuate. "Why don't people plan ahead?" he asks.

Back in the condo after dinner, alone. Ads in *Paradise News*: St. Pete Beach Realty.com. Spectacular Gulf views, $850,000. I'd like to see our accumulated family property wealth passed on to the kids but it looks like it won't be. Housing market will get worse. Tampa Bay Watch.org: they installed oyster domes to revive the bivalves…

The family bought a tile on the beach sidewalk that reads "Bird & Jean Thompson & family. Clarion PA to St. Pete Beach. Green woods to peaceful waters…" My parents' ashes are now part of the peaceful waters.

January 5

I meditate a while by the dunes, the sea oats. Look out at the blue watersky. It will look like this when the ocean is dead & covers the state. "From the stormy waves of birth, old age, sickness & death, from the ocean of samsara may I free all beings…" Open-eyed I let go of thoughts as they arise…

How does one free a jellyfish? Or a sandworm? A human? Try not to kill them. Pray for them to be reborn in the Pure Land of Amitabha, the Space of Great Bliss. They have minds; they have Buddha-nature…

Republicans take over the US House of Representatives at noon. Climate science deniers.

My cousin Jack & his wife Terri are coming. He calls. They're having traffic problems. He arrives with copies of an old photo of us boys at a camping trip. We were so skinny. Now Jack's legs hurt from bowling; Terri has an artificial knee. My knee not so good either.

After lunch, I ask my climate change questions. Jack responds. He thinks 2 inches for the sea level rise. He figures that only so much ice can melt so their place will be OK for a century. They would go to Tennessee if they had to move. A discussion follows. Property values will really fall says my cousin. I feel bad bringing up bad news to Jack & Terri. And not having a solution.

I get left off at Haslam's Bookstore, Florida's largest. But it's horrible. I'm greeted by Glenn Beck & George Bush in the entry display of books. No Buddhist books but plenty of Jesus stuff including a banner over the aisle that says something to the effect that Jesus is the only way to salvation. In the ecology section are a lot of denialists. But surprisingly, "The End of Nature" by Bill McKibben is there, plus James Lovelock's "The Revenge of Gaia." I've read that Lovelock's book is bleak. I read McKibben many years ago; it's great. To use my gift certificate from Sue, I choose *The Ninth: Beethoven and the World in 1824* by Harvey Sachs. I walk to Bob's. On his big TV there is PBS coverage of new speaker of the House, John Boehner.

*   *   *

Past, present & future. Why so little awareness of the future? I mean the future effects of causes. Like almost 7 billion humans burning carbon. The graph of CO2 in the air & the graph of temperature go higher together. Extrapolate, see the future. But the concept of karma, cause & effect, is difficult to grasp. We mostly think we can "get away" with bad behavior, that is, behavior which will cause suffering. The pervasiveness of suffering is also a hard concept. Impermanence is not too hard unless one applies it to one's own body. Death is something we don't like to think about much. The fourth of the four thoughts to turn one's mind toward enlightenment is that we have a rare opportunity to change for the better. Not only do most of us have a good brain but we have the possibility of connecting to enlightened beings to inspire us. For some, Jesus is the inspiration: blessed are the poor, the peacemakers... For me, it's my teachers, the wonderful lamas I have been blessed by. The Buddha.

The three times are dependent on each other. Therefore they have no independent existence.

The old photograph Jack gave me: I'm 16 or so, the tallest of the campers. Then there are Preston, my old friend; Jack; my Virginia brother, Jon; my nature-loving brother, Rick, from San Francisco. Dad took the picture; Bob was too little, stayed home with Mom & Sue. All I really remember is how cold the Hillsborough River was. All the changes since then. Fifty years of moments racing by, accumulating into habits, developing into writing, meditating, working. Jack could have become a songwriter; Preston could have been a professor. Causes & conditions at play. Illnesses: my bipolar, Jack's diabetes. Past, present & future in one moment.

I finish the book that Shannon's boyfriend, Aaron, gave me for Xmas. *Transcending Ego: Distinguishing Consciousness from Wisdom* by Thrangu Rinpoche. Pretty heady. Here's a quote: "The 5 external sensory consciousnesses are like a mute who can see. Although a mute person can see everything, he cannot describe what he has seen. The mental consciousness, on the other hand, is said to be like a blind person who can speak: he is able to describe things, but he cannot directly perceive them."

January 6

St. Petersburg Times, Jan. 6, 2011. "Panel: massive oil spill could happen again."

"Governor Rick Scott has appointed an executive of one of Florida's largest development companies to oversee the state department charged with managing growth... Scott also appointed a ship-building executive as his top environmental regulator... Nuclear plant to go online by April (Crystal River was shut down to repair cracks)."

"Cold leads to record for manatee deaths (767)" but total population is a record high of more than 5,000.

Preston comes over. I show him the photo. We're not skinny any more. We go out for lunch. I question him with my standard survey. His water comes from Lake Manatee reservoir; his power from Tampa's coal-fired plant. It owns coal fields in Kentucky he says. Sea level rise? No idea. He guesses 4 inches. He has flood insurance, thinks he & Connie have 60 years before house is uninhabitable. They would go to NC if they had to.

I tell him of positive feedback loops in progress & upcoming. I'm the climate doom man.

We go to Fort DeSoto State Park to look for birds & meet a pro birder. He says we saw redheads, a flock of rare ducks on the way out. We see white ibis, reddish egret, little blue heron, snowy egret, Wilson's plover, semipalmated plover, dunlins, sanderlings, woodstorks. The pro is looking for frigate birds but hasn't seen any. Preston mentions the black-bellied whistling ducks that are new in his pond. They are moving north with global warming. Audubon.com should be checked out.

Thanks, Preston, old friend. See you.

I eat dinner at a Thai place with Bob & Sue & David. I ask our waitress what the word for kindness is in Thai. She says it is tsaiDEE, good heart.

Bill McKibben's first book is called "The End of Nature." By the title he means that there is no longer a wild nature untouched by human-kind. The industrial revolution has permeated the earth with GHGs & other chemicals. The poles are warming faster than the rest of the planet. And the "third pole" of the Tibetan plateau, home to the compassionate teachings of the Buddha, is threatened too. What will happen to people in the valleys of the world when their glaciers & rivers dry up? If there was ever a time for "good heart" for all beings, this is it.

January 7

Good-hearted sister takes me to the airport. We hug goodbye. Who knows when or where or if we'll be together again? But maybe it's not my last trip to Florida. Maybe I'll wind up living here again out of economic necessity & I can help her with another Christmas jigsaw puzzle. And meditate on the waves. Impermanence. I love you. Call you tonight. Bye.

Chapter 2
High and Dry

Jan. 8

I'm back in Albuquerque. The Mile-High City.

I wake at 4, thirsty, having dreamed of getting angry at someone with a "one fucking track mind" trying to get me to pay some kind of fees. At 6 I'm done with my morning ngöndro. I'm back in the bag, a little short of breath.

Yesterday, at the Tampa airport I saw Andy, a chess player from Santa Fe. He beat me 2 games on his little portable board as we blasted through the sky westward.

Andy & I talked of global warming. He owns a Prius but flies all over the place just for fun. He mentioned the shift of the magnetic field too & pulled out a compass to follow our descent into ABQ.

Nap too long to get to phowa practice at Helen's. There's snow on South Sandia Peak. I pay $40 for a month of SpeedDate... Decide to have a car-free day. Chris returns my call & reports that Gov. Martinez has gone denialist already.

Jan. 9

Dreamed of playing "All You Need Is Love."

Read of nut with gun in AZ. 6 dead, 12 wounded including Rep. Gabrielle Giffords (D-AZ) with a bullet through her brain.

To Helen & Michael's for good talk by OR on TV. OR is our teacher, our lama from Tibet who now lives in Denver with his American wife. I'll just call him OR to respect his privacy. Samsara equals 3 types of suffering. Home to Eagles & Packers: suffering of suffering (pain of body, of losing), suffering of change (losing), pervasive suffering (all this...).

Jan. 10

Dream: rain, going to get in cab to work I get lost in the dark; meet others, build fire. Dog; barefoot. In real life, I'm a cab driver.

Physical therapy for knee cancelled; 10 days to next one.

Idea for song: "It's Hard," the 4 thoughts are hard to understand, but you can do it...

Back to work. Back in guzzler 448. It's cloudy & cold. First fare just in from Brazil. Earlier, I wrote R. & told her I had an extra room if she was too sick & tired to drive to Farmington after flight from CA. Thom Hartmann (TH) on my little radio I bring with me: he says the right wing is unrepentant about their shooting rhetoric, accuses left of violent rhetoric... Read of Beethoven, heroic creator. Truth/happiness. Effort/diligence.

Burning cold. Flee it home to pea soup & brownie for dinner. Brownies were a Christmas present from brother Jon in Virginia.

Jan. 11

Best sleep since coming back. Cold house, no cold water. Listen to Stephanie Miller on AZ. It's so depressing.

And back to work, driving taxi. Our Ford Crown Victorias get about 18 mpg. CoolBiz, a program of the Sierra Club, is going to contact our company, Albuquerque Cab, at my request. New York City has hybrid cabs; why not us? Unfortunately, our owner is old & a Christian Republican...

Our new governor has named climate science denier (& former astronaut) Harrison Schmitt to be head of the Energy, Minerals & Natural Resources Department. I say Harrison is full of Schmitt. He claimed environmentalists were communists.

Forgot my knee brace today. Also forgot bodhicitta. AH, my secret practice from APR. To do a few minutes a day.

Mirror-like wisdom see aging face in mirror. AH. Everybody dies in samsara, illusory samsara. AH. Been here before: blue at airport, thinking nothing has changed! Text from Shannon: she's cooking. Temporary happiness. NPR: family of shooter statement; Giffords improving! Cute girl in Whole Foods.

Jan. 12

Dreams. Get to bank after walk. Need to work.

Idea for song: get real, here's the deal, she'll never give you the time of day, she'll never feel the way you do, get real, turn the wheel, no matter how you feel, she'll never kiss your blues away...

*   *   *

12

Samsara equals the 3 types of suffering. Suffering of suffering, e.g. it's too cold. Suffering of change, e.g. it was OK in Florida but now it's cold. All-pervasive suffering, e.g. just being alive...

The Buddha's teaching is like the sun shining through clouds; People of Tingri, now is the one time it is present.

—Padampa Sangye

In cab at elementary school, waiting. Kids come by on their way to the cafeteria. Look, it's a taxi! They wave & smile. Boys, I was like you once, agog in a sea of beauty.

Shannon text: needs money. Call her: she's down, groggy. I'm glad I have a good way of waking up in the morning & doing dharma practice. Lynn's car damaged by careless driver on ice. Ben & Em are visiting.

One year ago today, 230,000 Haitians died in the earthquake. Listening to Randi Rhodes makes me want to picket KKOB for airing Rush the Lying Lie-bagger. I get mad talking about it with a passenger. She agrees with me fortunately. Lots of time to read of Beethoven's age. Then Palin with her "blood libel" remarks. She of the crosshairs on democratic seats. It's always about her, poor Sarah.

Om Ami Dewa Hri. May APR live long, benefiting countless beings, bringing them to enlightenment.

Home to Barack Obama in Tucson. So moving, so Bodhisattva-like. I cry for Christina, the dead 9 year old girl (& others). Jumping in puddles in heaven.

Jan. 13

Body, speech & mind: light...

It's too late, it's too bad, it's too hot, it's too sad, she was bright, she was cool, well alright, you're a fool —samsara. Slight headache all day. Precious human lifetime some moments; some moments of affliction. Sunset like that of peaceful Mesa San Luis where brother Rick & Gloria & I camped last October.

Home: Rick calls. He has doubts about clean coal. Then Sue calls while I'm meditating.

Jan 14

Wake to Beethoven. Wow. Write Tom Lyons & give him Climateprogress.org. (CP) Wash dishes to Beethoven's 9th—doesn't sound like despair to me in first movement.

USA Today, big ad: Prepare for Global Warming. It's only an ad for the Golden Globes. There's a push for drones to police US skies... NPR: Tunisian president quits due to protests. Man set himself on fire. Copycats in other Arab countries.

Postcarbon.org. The future looks...challenging.

Saturday, Jan. 15

I sleep in till 7:35. Walk good. Knee better for sure. Not perfect though. SPACE...

Sue: gorgeous day in FL.

I try new song. It's pretty basic, needs complex bridge of "get real." Wake up, think straight, it's way too late. Someone will give, you reason to live. The only way, is get real today...

Feeling bipolar with alternating slow days. Steelers–Ravens. I get my mala to make it more meaningful, pray for players, crowd. Write a bit. Car-free day. Comfort zone.

Jan. 16

Awakened at 4:45 by dream: beautiful college girl on bed with me flirts as I write on back of a welcome mat...

Guru Yoga. Green Tara practice at Copper Mountain, APR's meditation center in Corrales, with Carol. OR video with Helen. Foods. Jets. Tunisia. CP. Eyes tired.

Jan. 17

MLK Day. Wake early with a Rainbow Gathering dream. That leads to the singing of my Black Elk song, "A Sacred Voice" which I wrote in 1973.

TH: he has absolute faith we can turn it around. I am uncertain, but teachers speak of "degenerate times." When do we hit bottom? Enlightenment possible for some even in the midst of civil unrest, food shortages. I have faith in rebirth too.

Good day in cab. Home to call Chris Rawlins. He won't go to a doctor, says diabetes is his bad karma. He says he's worked so hard at healing himself through mantras & still is getting worse. Wrong view? Sad for him & angry too. Sit a bit. Bed at 8:30.

Jan. 18

Email to R.: I'll take morning of the 26th off to have breakfast with you.

Finish *The Ninth* by Harvey Sachs. Great book! In the bullpen, where cabs park to go wait at the airport. It has to be 60 degrees. Working on "Real." Sun behind Sheraton now & it's cooler.

Energy, Minerals & Natural Resources Department head for NM? Climate science denier, Harrison Schmitt?

Give Adrianna a copy of my CD, *Now Here This*. She's a girl at the cab office. Home to BBC, "A Sacred Voice," "Get Real," guitar out of tune.

Jan. 19

Dreams of kids, playing guitar. Wake at 3:30 with "Blues in the Bottle" by the Holy Modal Rounders. Drift back to sleep? Sweet Schubert on now.

At the mercy of history & economy.

Pick up nurse D. Ph.D. banjo player buys a CD from me! We exchange cards. I was listening to *All That Jazz* on KUNM & she liked it. She mentions Rodney Crowell being a great songwriter & a Buddhist & coming to town.

"Hard to Get" (title). Freedom, rare life. Nothing is permanent. Cause & effect. So much pain. Do you get it? It's hard to get…

Office: Adrianna says CD is awesome, is playing it for the whole office.

Jan. 20

Dream of Dawa, my old dog I had to put to sleep & do phowa for. She came back from running off.

To PT with Sandy Knudsen. I put on shorts so she can watch my knee as I walk & squat. She shows me stretches, puts icepack on it. Next appointment in 2 weeks unless it resolves on its own.

R.: plane in at 11:19, lunch. I try to think how to work & still see her. But "she'll never feel the way I feel."

Mallards at regular customer, Dori's, apartments. CP: millions of birds killed interacting with humans every year. I take old Dori & her autistic son to Walmart, as usual. She's into Edgar Cayce etc. I took her to see OR once. TH: honeybee democracy, choosing nest sites, like neurons in brain says Thomas Sealey. Pick up a guy from Tucson who's in the same synagogue as Gabby Giffords. She is recovering.

In 14 years I'll be 81; Shannon, 37. Earth will be in big doo-doo, if we live that long. R. on mind; she's so pretty & a Buddhist. Also, my age. I wrote a song for her called "Why I'm in Love with You" with only the slightest feedback from her that she liked me sort of. Hopeless romantic, get real.

Obama 2012: first bumpersticker. D. again—kind of cute. A wacky lady claims there are wolves all over NM. She used to live in Chimayo with bears, lions & eagles.

"Get Real"

Get real, no deal, you don't appeal
She's sweet, she's nice, but for love no dice
She'll never feel the way you feel
She'll never feel the way you feel

It's hot, it's late, it's not that great
Get real, right now, do you know how?
She'll never feel the way you feel
She'll never feel the way you feel

Wake up, think straight, it's way too late
There's just one way, get real today
She'll never feel the way you feel
She'll never feel the way you feel

Get really really really real

R. said once that she'd be my girlfriend & then changed her mind & wanted more time. Then we met in Santa Fe & on the way up to see the golden aspens, I held her hand for a minute. But she wasn't into it. She just wanted to be friends…but that wasn't to be, either. Oh well. I got a couple of good songs out of her.

Jan. 21

I try stretches & no ibuprofen. But walking around the block hurts. Is it too early for PT? Brother Rick warned me.

"Interview with a Dakini" posted by Maxim on Facebook. Bodhicitta & emptiness. She's an oracle with the Dalai Lama. Wow. Inspiring.

Randi: "good news"—Gabby on her way to Houston hospital— economy to recover this year—wait, is that good? Is that true? Is there another bump up before the postcarbon slide?

Happy robins in bullpen trees. Not making much money today. Light at the end of the week. A stunning beauty applying to be a psych intern. I pick her up twice.

Saturday, Jan. 22

I had to pay $150 for psych meds—am I in donut hole on my Medicare? Time to go get Nick, my new tech guy, who I met at Copper Mountain through Carol. He was there to work for her, not to meditate. We go to Olympia Cafe for Greek food. He has a solar scientist friend. We record 4 songs then I take him home (he has no car).

ABC TV News: Deep Freeze in US. Why? They don't say. Is it because Arctic is warm? Also, Giffords, straw poll in NH for fascists.

Need a break from doom? Try guru yoga!

Jan. 23

Three kayas (bodies). Can't get internet. "Rainbow in Curved Air" plays. Granola. Hung hung hung. Lost my APR necklace when string came untied. Where will it turn up, if at all? Fortunately, I have another one (though not as good). Reputed to be a good protection from sudden death...

I call Nick who says just to unplug power.

*   *   *

More from ecobuddhism.org.

125,000 cattle slaughtered every day in the US. Vegetarians cause less global warming.

The top 10 composers according to Anthony Tommasini at NYT: Bach, Beethoven, Mozart, Schubert, Debussy, Stravinsky, Brahms, Verdi, Wagner & Bartok.

I talk to Sue. I shy away again from advising her to sell her condo on the beach. Maybe brother Rick will sell his first. The properties have lost 40% of their value. Or maybe they take the losses. Somebody will lose. Last night I read about CH4 emissions from East Siberian Continental Shelf & the potential for abrupt climate change. "The rapid release to the atmosphere of methane trapped in permafrost & on continental margins" was among "four types of abrupt change in the paleoclimatic record that stand out as being so rapid & large in their impact that if they were to recur, they would pose clear risks to society in terms of our ability to adapt." (US Global Change Research Program report, "Abrupt Climate Change") I should write to the paper about Gov. Martinez.

NFL. Plus birds of paradise dancing in New Guinea forests. How long?

Jan. 24

Dreams of camping with Rick.

Put on new (old) APR medallion. As French toast cooks I listen to "Offering" which Nick sent me, my song offering. Do my stretches before walk.

First fare reports on shifting magnetic field. I'm reading *Confident Death* again, OR's book.

In 2035, when I die (haha), things on earth will be stressful. Practice being calm now. We need to become very calm. And very kind.

The mountain emerges

From a pink snow cloud

Hovers like a granite hawk over the city

D. has nice skin. Irish. Says she'll listen to *Now Here This* tonight. Impermanence of life.

Jan. 25

May the precious Bodhicitta which has not arisen arise, that has arisen not be broken & may it continually increase! Do it in Tibetan too.

Leg not twitching, headache gone, but another slow day in the taxi business. Anxiety about money. Should I help Shannon buy a car? Customer Carole & I talk doom. She's an environmental attorney, knows people. I give her a CD, then she buys it.

NM Supreme Court gives enviros victory: governor can't repeal law on GHGs from previous administration. Obama's State of the Union speech talks about "winning the future" & energy efficiency but he includes as clean energy gas, coal & nukes. And he never uses the terms "climate" or "warming." Climate Progress analysis.

Jan. 26

Email from R.: Whoops! Fog in CA, can't meet for lunch. She might rent a car & drive instead of fly, even though she feels sick. I send Shanny $100. Radio: Egyptian demonstrations. More snow in NE. Ad: Rocky Mozell says give a star for Valentine's Day. (I fell for it one Christmas & named one "Bird & Jean Thompson" as a gift for my parents—a very dim star in Lyra) TH: fascist strategy is to keep economy bad so they can win in 2012. AH. Work is slow again.

Letter in the *Alibi* newspaper, from me: "Gubernatorial Flatulence—Dear *Alibi*, Thanks for the article "Guv Sued Over Eco Rules: (News, Jan. 20–26.). Life on Earth faces the overwhelming threats of global warming & ocean acidification due to human releases of greenhouse gases. Business as usual just doesn't cut it anymore. But Martinez is clearly in the pocket of big business & against environmental regulations. What do we have to do? Impeach her?"

Stupid paper thinks it's funny with that title for the letter. Oh well.

Egypt: 700 arrests. Mubarak has ruled for 30 years. Fire, symbol of anger.

PBS: Foxo gene for longevity is in worms & humans.

Jan. 27

Dreams: stupa, a naked female.

Sit in chair rather than on floor; both knees ache now. Too much sitting cross-legged.

Sea level rise. 6 feet in 90 years; 1 foot in 15 yrs.—if it's linear (& it's not). It will be exponential.

Philip Glass drove a cab in NY City (even as his opera was at the Met). Fellow Buddhist.

#35, David, got an ornithology textbook for 25 cents. Birds' sex organs atrophy to save weight when they're not mating. David says he'd

like to come back as a bird. I say they have short, hard lives. A fundamentalist Jew from Israel is worried about Egypt. Bearded fear: you can't
negotiate with terrorists he says.

Jan. 28

Dreams of endless celebrations include APR, who says "I am the
stock market." I'm trying to give away food but everyone is fed. At one
point, I think woman is APR but she's his sister or someone else beautiful.

Should I title this book *A Buddhist's View of the Future? Farewell
Florida—A Buddhist's Reflections on Global Warming, Peak Everything &...?*

I see a honeybee! I'm in shirtsleeves at work, with the AC on.
Om Ami Dewa Hri. One of the mantras I can do while driving. It's for
the dead & for the long life of APR.

Egypt causing oil to go up to $90 a barrel; Dow down 166. El Ba-
radei speaks; Mubarak speaks, asks his government to resign. Home to
turn on Egyptian action on BBC when Shannon calls. Phone bill again. I
try to cheer her up about buying a car halvsies with Aaron, her boyfriend.
Brave Egyptians up against armed dictator.

Here is the prayer I say before bed usually. It was composed by
APR on Jan. 7, 2007.

> *"Spontaneous Occurence of All Wishes: An Aspirational
> Prayer for Extreme Times"*
>
> *Namo Ratna Trayaya (homage to the Three Jewels)*
>
> *I bow down before the gurus, buddhas & bodhi-
> sattvas of the past, present & future & in all ten direc-
> tions. I present them with offerings. I go to them for refuge.
> I entreat them to bless me with empowering inspiration.
> Based on these roots of virtue, may I & all limitless sen-
> tient beings, in all of our lifetimes, meet authentic mentors
> —friends in virtue who will show us the path. May we
> take birth in excellent bodies —supporting all eight free-
> doms & ten advantages; may we naturally have the power
> to bring about our own aims & to benefit others; may we
> have the power to place all wandering beings in an ocean of
> bliss & happiness. May Buddha's precious Teachings —
> the scriptures & the realizations —come to be perceived in
> true harmony by all, without bias or sectarianism. May the*

Buddha's Teachings —their explanation & their accom-plishment —spread throughout space. May disasters such as illness, famine, war & the destruction of our environ-ment cease to exist right on the spot. May all enjoy the glo-rious happiness & well-being of past eras. May it be equal to that in the Blissful Pure Land of Amitabha. May all sentient beings who have passed away & are newly in the intermediate state between death & rebirth—especially (here insert the name(s) of those you wish to remember) — not have experienced the suffering of a traumatic death. May their hallucinations in the intermediate state cease to exist right on the spot; may they be transported to the pure land of Sukhavati, the Joyous. In summary, may all wan-dering sentient beings —who have all been our mothers— come to achieve their aims without impediment in any way or at any time. May they come to be like Siddhartha, our Buddha—"He Who Achieved All Aims." These aspira-tional prayers have been sown in order to create circum-stances conducive to their realization. Through the power of the Three Jewels—our source of refuge—& the power of the truth of the inevitability of actions (karma) & their ef-fects, may these aspirations be achieved!

Tayata Pandzati Awabodana Ye Soha
(third, revised translation —Jan. 10, 2008 by
Khedrup Sangpo)

Jan. 29

Myriad displays; some confusion in dreams & life.

Wrote D. & heard back: she wants to go see Rodney Crowell with me. I like her voice. How young is she? How young am I? She's younger than I am, I know that.

Egypt: protesters & Army (not police) are friendly.

Car-free day. Bed at 8.

Jan. 30

Up at 5. Dzogchen moments. D. replies with cell# & emaho ("wonderful").

Nicholas Kristof in *NYTimes*: 80 dead per day in US to guns. Hubble space photos. Adagio, Beethoven's 9th. So beautiful.

Call D. She enjoyed listening to my CD, especially "Ah." She is amazing. Doesn't practice formally but reads about B-ism. She named her cats "Bodhi" & "Citta." We walk with crows along Rio Grande by Bridge St. She was born the year I got out of high school. Lots of experiences, never married (like me).

Now it's "when" not "if" Mubarak goes. Sixth day of protests. El Baradei spoke to thousands. Boehner praises Obama. Al Jazeera in Egypt shut down. Children in Pakistan malnourished.

Sue calls. She has to read depositions before bed. Hard working Public Defender.

Jan. 31

Winter storm warning. Back hurts. Two sweet emails from the D.: a poem & thankyou & bodhicitta. Wow. Cottonwood Buddha Devotees speaking the language of "Emaho"! I wonder if she knows how old I am. I'm almost 67! (an old crow) Also one from R.: she drove straight through, didn't stop here, very sick.

Lester Brown. 350. Make a stand wherever you live but be ready to move. No more BAU. Learn phowa, the meditation for death. Cut carbon footprint. Ready.gov for giant snowstorm. Not feeling well, achy, tired. Bed early tonight; it's all relative truth. Raining a bit. Now snow. World impermanent. Home to lie down, eat, lie down, sit, lie down, dream.

Feb. 1

Dream of Rainbow Gathering. Lonely anyway in crowd. Girl helps me. Map of site: it's near a 22,000 foot peak & the town of "Blur." Up at 5. Snow on ground. Jesus! I fall on the way back from School Board election. I'm OK. No school today. It's snowing again; streets icy. Funny how I still say the name of Jesus sometimes even though I've been a Buddhist so long. God, too. Well, I believe in Jesus. But not God.

*   *   *

Massive snowstorm stretches from NM to MA. Historic proportions. It will affect 110 million people. I watch NBC TV: jet stream way south.

In cab at Lomas & Girard. Blowing snow. Roads snow-packed & icy.

In love so many times. Infatuated. Infatuated with the fatuous imagination. And then there is the reality of D.. Call, leave message.

Mubarak says he won't seek reelection in September. Protesters: go now. Surveillance in Egypt by phones. Rising food prices causing unrest. Jordan's king feeling the pressure. World food price index at a record high.

11 degrees. 4 to 8 inches of snow predicted for tonight.

As I'm finishing my Brussels sprouts, D. calls. She'd left message in the early afternoon too. I think we're in love. She speaks German & Swahili. I say I just speak English. She says I speak B-ism.

Usually I turn the heater off before bed to save gas. Not tonight.

Feb. 2

Dream that some new supervisor wants me to work a night shift. No way. Also, I'm late for dinner with #35.

Pro-Mubarak mobs are now attacking protesters in Tahrir Square. No new snow; that's a nice surprise. Sonnenschein. Facebook: donothingfor2minutes.com. Try it. It's a meditation.

It was zero degrees at 6. Should I go out for my walk? I'm well-fed & warm. No, it's too breezy; I lie down. Go to bank but it's closed. Go to work.

Temperatures from *USA Today*: Barrow, 6 -3; Fairbanks, 13 7; Nome, 12 8; ABQ, 13 -1. Yesterday.

Democracy Now: Thugs are police out of uniform & oil workers. Attacking peaceful demonstrators.

I get dispatched to D's. Oh boy! She has to teach before the concert. A nice sundog by the sun. It's 5 degrees; going to -11 tonight.

Home to eat the usual, watch BBC. Then pick up D. at UNM & go to the concert at the National Hispanic Cultural Center. Burning cold. She asks about my teacher, then Rodney Crowell sings & picks & reads from his memoir of crazy parents. His melodies aren't that great but lyrics are down to earth. No indication that he's a Buddhist. (D. saw him before at B-ist benefit in NYC). I give him a CD & he says he'll listen to it. Frigid. Hold hands briefly.

Feb. 3

Sleep from 10:30 to 4:30. EMAHO! I'm at Central & Louisiana before the cab heater kicks in. Himalayas to the east.

Electronic sign says natural gas shortage in NM! I hope not at my house... Turn my little radio to the rightwing station that at least has local news (unlike the progressive station). Something about rolling blackouts in Texas due to record cold. Some towns like Bernalillo have no gas & people are going to shelters to stay warm.

Home to gas! Also messages from D. & Shanny. Lovely daughter has propane, no need for shelter. I call brother Rick. He saw 8 California condors at Pinnacles. 70 degrees in San Francisco, no rain.

Feb. 4

13 degrees. I go for a walk so I don't lose muscle.

10:21, waiting for Dori. Her pond is frozen & the ducks have flown away. Her full name is Doris Curtain. She & her son to Walmart as usual. The paper says there are 32,000 people with no heat in NM. State of emergency says governor. Angel Fire & Eagle's Nest went down to minus 36 degrees. It's unknown when all the gas will be back on.

I think it was triage: to cut off Taos, etc. to save ABQ & Santa Fe. The cold increased demand for energy in TX plus caused decreased production of CH_4. It's a vicious circle: global warming/extreme weather causes more demand for energy causes more global warming/extreme weather.

Pick up Dori & David again. My trunk is full of Hawaiian punch, chips, bottled water. I think about D. Journalists being attacked by Mubarak. Bad apartment house fire in city. I can see the black smoke from Walmart.

Home. Breathe. Rick calls: has his year all planned out, including backpacking in the Gila in October. Too tired to call D.

Saturday, Feb. 5

D. has a bad cough, from a parasite she picked up in Africa as a college student.

24,000 people still without gas; 75 homeless from fire.

Song idea: "When You Have a Girlfriend" (there's hardly time for anything) But do I really have a girlfriend?

Nick comes over after we go to Olympia Cafe again. Record "You Were in my Heart" on his portable device. Then to D's. Two hour talk. She's coming down with something. She went to work at age 4, picking strawberries. Played banjo too. Lived with a pot dealer in NYC for ten years but never could get high. We tell stories of families, borderlines & all. Little hug goodbye.

Feb, 6

D. writes it was a "saintly hug;" she cancelled her trip to DC because of illness. I am definitely not a saint.

Call Sue: her friend may have cancer. She's taking her old twirling baton to the Super Bowl party.

Oh no! Another CP email! "Be embraced, you millions..." from "Ode to Joy." Then to phowa practice & a web teaching from OR. Next: Santa Fe. National Anthem sung by Christina Aguilera. And the Super Bowl is under way. Christine makes naan & beans. Chris Worth comes over. The two Chrises drink beer; Green Bay wins. An ad mentioning Tibet. Chris thinks it's exploitative. I say it's great to even hear about Tibet on the Super Bowl.

Feb. 7

D. has to think about going to see OR with me...

Cab karma. OR says it's a good way to make a living, to support my dharma practice. So many people, rich & poor. OR from the web teaching: we see suffering as happiness, impermanence as permanence... So, we see precious human life as ordinary life, karma as random. What delusion! Om Ah Hung.

Get stuck in snow in Zuzax, at Liston's. His mom died at age 98 the other day & he's sentimental about it. He's blind, his son not all there, his wife OK I guess. They sit in the cab as I spin deeper into the cold mud. I'm feeling clear, tell the blind man not to worry, remember what Jesus said. He says he's a nervous wreck. Finally Bob comes from the office & pushes us out & I take them to Smith's for food shopping.

Home now, chocolate. Tired. Should I call D.? I do, leave message.

Feb. 8

Rainbow dreams. But I'm lonely. Nothing from D. Start thinking that it's only platonic & saintly on her side. D. is for dukngal (suffering)? Maybe. I feel the need for "healthy attachment". She "owes me" an email & call. So I'll wait & do the same old job.

Largest crowd yet in Cairo. Pick up D. in cab. We talk, I'm nervous, disconnected. She tips me & says she'll see me soon. Later, a vet from the VA says he can't breathe. But he can. He's a racist, going to San Diego to see his daughter. On the bus. Good luck.

Home. D. calls. Wants to dine out. Mentions our friendship, relationship, says I'm very patient. CP: Amazon drought really bad. It could become a carbon emitter rather than a carbon sink.

Feb. 9

My *ngondro* is infiltrated with thoughts. Nice email from D. on where to eat.

TH is now #8 talker in US (behind 7 fascists). Gabby speaks! OK gets more snow. I do tonglen practice in the cab. It's using breath to take in suffering & send out happiness. Until I pick up Tara. She's 19, sexy, big, fair, with a nose-ring. She's moving into the Women's Hospital after being evicted from Ronald McDonald House for disagreement with another woman. She has a premature baby in the hospital, lots of stuff to move. I help her. Much sexier than D. Get real!

Home to CP: Chinese drought threatens wheat; floods in South Africa threaten food production there.

D. Calls & leaves message as I meditate but I'm too tired to call back. New sleep/death prayer I make up: may I live & die with mindfulness...

Feb. 10

Wake at 5, my own old songs in head...

Don't let the perfect be the enemy of the good. Tara is perfect? Haha. Cold walk.

2,000 days with ABQ Cab approximately. If spent doing dharma practice I'd be broke but clear...Probably with fewer aches. Myriad appearances in mind. A lot of waiting for fares. Gas at $3.09 a gallon.

Maybe I shouldn't have eaten that sandwich; guts hurt. I could fast in the evenings.

Not feeling romantic now that's for sure. Signs of living organism: irritability, tropism, i.e. aversion & attraction.

Anger in Cairo after Mubarak says he'll stay till September. Rocky Mozell: name a star after D. for Valentine's Day. I call her. The pipes at her work burst from the cold & she had to evacuate. I tell her I'm too sick to dine. She's sweet, for sure. I wonder if worrying about seeing her tonight caused my intestines to freak out.

Yogurt for dinner. Watch "Clever Monkeys" on PBS. Troop sleeping together on a branch; tool use, murder.

Feb. 11

Harrison Schmitt backs out of post with Martinez, says he didn't like the background investigation. Emaho!

Shanny calls! She's going to Denver with Aaron for a zen sword-fighting thing. I ask her if she needs money; she only has $50.

Mubarak RESIGNS! Non-violent revolution! Military in charge. Happy Egyptians celebrate their 7,000 year history. Obama: non-violent power for justice. Sweet! Suleiman out too (the torturer). September 11, 2001 to February 11, 2011: Muslim evolution. 32 years ago was the Iranian Islamic revolution. More news: jobs needed just to keep up with population growth.

Texas church-goer in cab wasn't excited by the news from Egypt, probably fears Muslims. But D. was! She loaned me a CD of Egyptian singer she got when she was there; she had on her Egyptian necklace. We went to Orchid Thai; she looked beautiful, such good skin. She talked the most: she's going to Navajo Nation next weekend where she's been so many times. She plans to get a car by March. We hold hands for a minute before she goes in to crash from staying up late again last night working.

Saturday, Feb. 12

NYTimes: "Egypt Erupts in Jubilation as Mubarak Steps Down." Sign email to D. "love." Four years since my last lover, Linda.

Jan. 2011 globally is tied for 10th warmest in history despite cold in US. I search through dusty notebooks of crazy writing. Find "Fool's Paradise" original, the story of 1973 trip out west.

My fortune from Orchid Thai: "Soon someone new coming into your life will be a best friend." To stores listening to smooth rhythms of Amr Diab. Home now, ripping CD to computer, with door open. It feels warmer that predicted 51.

Write. Time warp of 38 years. Autobiographical anxiety, lying in bed after dinner. Or is it love anxiety? Call D., leave message.

Feb. 13

4:30 wake up with dry mouth & new melody in my head. Get up & write it down. Sleep again; up at 7:45. Nothing from D. Would have to rush to get to Copper Mountain & my heart isn't in it today. Goji berries, tea & guru yoga. Then call Sue. Their dog, Cinderella, died. Put to sleep yesterday. They were up all night with her last week, poor unhappy Cinder.

Print up "Get Real," another song for my book of song lyrics. Another CD possible? Work on "Fool's." It's going to be a no car day, no shower day, unless I hear from D. I'm making up stuff for "Fool's" to create reality of me 38 years ago, the end section of my diary from then which I didn't finish. I was in dear, dirty Boston on Feb. 13, hippie delusion going strong.

I take a break to get some sun on my torso. D. calls. She is a rape survivor. It happened 12 years ago. Her therapist is her teacher, therefore she's not much into Buddhism! She's not into a physical thing with me but we can become good friends. Her Ph.D. is in anthropology. I think to myself that maybe we could just hug…

Feb. 14

Ngondro plus Medicine Buddha for D. My neck hurts. Mockingbird in spruce down the street. 53 degrees at 9:15. 1973 on my mind. Go to work. Work is slow. After 4 hours, a measly $27 on meter, $10 in tips. Very nice day. 65 degrees at 5. Total book for day: $110. Oh yeah, it's Valentine's Day.

Feb. 15

Radio wake up: "Gymnopédie #1" by Satie. Timeless melody. UFO video from Maxim. 8 degrees above normal. Bahrain square taken by demonstrators; big protest in Tehran.

28

another sun
appears in a little white cloud
disappears into space

*   *   *

New Mexico carbon footprint is the same as the country of Finland. That's because we burn coal for other states at the Four Corners plants. We must shrink it nonetheless. (Florida CO2 output is that of Thailand & Latvia combined.) (Thanks to *Sierra* magazine, January–February 2011.)

"It was said by Buddha Shakyamuni that to work for beings with kindness & compassion, & to make offerings to the Buddhas are of equal value for the attainment of enlightenment." —Dilgo Khyentse Rinpoche

Feb. 16

To my counselor, Jon. Tell him about 350, etc. He volunteers at Nature Center with birds of prey. What do I do? Talk & write. Who reads? Also, drive a cab.

TH: author of "Overdiagnosed." Tests can almost always find something wrong with a person. Some "early sign of death" as OR would say. But treating can be a problem & costly.

Dreamed last night that Dad wanted to see a Presbyterian counselor & I helped in some way.

Feb. 17

Nick emails; he's done an hour of work on how to promote my music. Various comments on FB to my status: "tax the obscenely rich." Eternal recurrence in cab driving. Kiss the joy as it flies & the rest of it too (the sadness).

Bahrain king attacks protesters. Wisconsin fascists attack public employees; tens of thousands protest there. Democratic senators walk out of the legislature in Madison.

I cancel SpeedDate, get $39.95 back. 20 dead in Libyan protest.

Dry, itchy ankles bug me.

Sexual harassment common in Egypt —except during the protests.

A fare who is an Endangered Species Act lawyer.

Feb. 18

Brother Rick's birthday 57.

11:30 Just dropped off Finnish exchange student at airport. Platinum blonde, white skin, black boots, red coat. I hummed "Finlandia" by Jean Sibelius for her. She was texting a lot; a teenager. If only you were mine & we could text each other…

Can I be mindful during daily life? When desire arises? In dreams? How about in dying?

I start reading "Penetrating Wisdom" by Dzogchen Ponlop Rinpoche.

Trazadone, 100 mg before bed. Should I mess with it? Some dizziness, difficulty in waking up in the morning.

Call Nick, make an appointment for tomorrow. What will I record? "Alesya," "You're Killing Me," "Could You Be My Girl?" & "Get Real."

Saturday, Feb. 19

Dreamed I was trying to teach Chenrezi practice to Rick & Sue in 10 minutes. Kept getting interrupted. Woke during mantra of Om mani padme hung at 3 am.

"The nonconceptual experience of rigpa, the flash of the wisdom of rigpa, is constantly interrupted." —Dzogchen Ponlop Rinpoche. You can say that again. Between thoughts is inconceivable wisdom.

Life expectancy at birth in US is 78.24 years. That will change.

Nick Kristof tweet: "Wow! I'm awed to watch the courage of Bahrainis. Such guts. And it worked: they have reclaimed a place stained with blood."

After buying pills at Costco (cheaper this time) & a haircut, I go home to croak songs. Then pick up Nick & we go to Annapurna. Record only 2 songs before tiring.

5:30 ABC TV news. Wisconsin story leads. March 4 deadline on budget in Washington. The news is slanted toward conflict. Ads for drugs, oil & gas. Nano drone.

AH

Feb. 20

No sun. Gloomy but there is light from Guru Rinpoche. Will go see OR pixels today plus, hopefully, D. Maybe we could go to a movie. First, get out of bed again & wash dishes.

D. calls, talks of her grant proposal to interview nurses in NM. She coughs, wants to lay low today.

I call Sue. A friend's husband died suddenly. Bob's ex's daughter in jail for drugs. Vinny stopped smoking. Kelly's baby will be born March 11; to be named Avery.

My daughter on FB: emotions. I get anxious about her. Sit, call, text with no response.

"Kadak" means alpha-purity. "Spontaneously arising luminosity, lhundrup, is present right from the beginning." —DPR

Feb. 21

Last page of this notebook. Last notebook? No way. I write to live, live to die. Live for bodhicitta for all beings, including Amber Harris who wrote a letter to the paper on climate change. Last few words to try to describe the undescribable. Can't even describe the relative phenomena let alone the absolute. Kadak doesn't stop when I close my eyes. Or when I talk to a fare. Or start, anytime.

I pick up Bob Anderson of Stop the War Machine. They're protesting on March 19.

Home in time for BBC News: tours of Kate Middleton's hometown. Then anxious sitting. Lonely, to bed at 9.

Feb. 22

A beautiful female lama on FB, in Spain. NRDC: at least 17 aborted or stillborn dolphins have washed up on the Gulf Coast this year.

I call Chris: he & Christine are going to Crested Butte, skiing. He signs off with "Bodhi Dharma," a little dharma joke.

Then I pick up Monica. She's originally from Poland; now lives in Florida. She's trying to get a NM driver's license to save money on FL's fees. Love that Slavic accent. Moanika. Waiting time adding up. WWBD? CNN Radio: Hillary says bloodshed unacceptable in Libya; Ghaddafi says he will die a martyr; Ohio says it's broke (the GOP mantra & they caused it). Still with cutie, Monika. She's trying to borrow a car from somebody to take a road test with. I told her she couldn't use the cab...She's got one! A bride-to-be tries on a wedding dress; a crazy girl shakes her hands wildly & screams. Meter is up to $67. She has a nice body but smokes. All illusory. Focus on the top of the head. Advice to practice from OR.

Now Monica doesn't need to take the test after all. Polska goes back to airport. I give her my card. She has a boyfriend.

More driving, then home to BBC. I skip Climate Progress. I call Norma, at the stupa in Santa Fe. She's sad because Lama Dorje has ordered all the big Siberian elms cut down. He thinks they are destroying pipes. The good news is that there is a new lama living there: Lama Mingma Sherpa. I want to say I love you instead of goodbye but I don't.

Feb. 23

Little nightmare. Shannon in it & Dawa. I listen to Rachmaninoff on the radio. Incredible. Guru yoga. Inspired.

New York Times: "Oil Soars as Libyan Furor Shakes Markets." Gasoline at $3.19 per gallon.

R. emails. Wants to do a retreat with me at Tara Mandala. I reply with my dharma plan for the summer. My plan doesn't include Tara Mandala however. It's exciting to think she likes me enough to want that.

Americans trying to get out of Libya. Obama condemns Ghaddafi. Namo, O-Man.

I work late with crazy woman who crashes her shopping cart into the side of the cab. Poor thing. Just a scratch on cab but I get her info in case boss sees the scratch. She tips big.

Feb. 24

Beauty of Christine, the cover model on a make-up brochure sent to Elizabeth Thompson at my address. Pink & white & gold. Beauty of mallard on Dori's pond. Green, iridescent. Beauty of clouds in sky. White & blue. Moral beauty of protesters in Madison, Libya. No color.

TH: Oxytocin healing from kissing. Now there's an idea. Who will kiss me?

Bad weather keeps 100 Americans in Tripoli port. Military option for US in Libya weighed.

I'm thinking of taking off from work in the summer & driving to CO for OR retreats. With R.? With Shannon? GW: global warming. OA:

ocean acidification. PE: peak everything. What to do about them? Write, meditate.

Democracy Now. Bradley Manning held in solitary for 9 months now. Report from free East Libya. Koch brothers' father was co-founder of John Birch Society. Gov. Walker of WI is a stealth fascist. Ghaddafi says revolt caused by hallucinogens.

Feb. 25

Dreams…news…*kyerim…dzogrim*…eggs…news…walk…play…airport…thank goodness it's Friday.

Nothing back from R. I'm resentful I have to work. Lonely.

Bullpen "party," lots of drivers. I talk to #35 about death, climate change. He'd rather talk about his favorite TV show.

Get busy, no time to write. End up making some money.

Feb. 26

Dream that I'm trying to tell Mom & Dad about peak oil. Family all there. Dad is lighting incense. An old stump on fire. I'm trying to play a 2-string instrument with a plectrum, which I lose. Somehow I keep jamming. Is it with Doug? I wake with my mouth dry at 5:21.

I think I'll call my next CD *Prayer Wheel* instead of *Offering*. I will try to do it cheaply, not like the first one which I spent $7000 on. See, it spins & it has some dharma in it. Not as much as a real prayer wheel but…

Usual Saturday gut problems in spite of D's recommended peppermint oil. I forward Climate Progress email to brother Rick-Dave. My get up & go has got up & went…

Feb. 27

Wake to chorus of the Ninth. Joy! To Copper Mountain; to Nick's. Record 5 songs. Feel good.

Hillary in Geneva; Ghaddafi's son says everything is OK. Sue calls. Oscars till 8.

Feb. 28

Check from work. $442.17 for 10 days (that's $44 per day) plus tips ($20 average) = $8/ hour.

Mohammed from nursing home (he works there). He has questions about B-ism even though he's a Muslim. He's only 21.

R. calls! Amazing. Her root teacher is Trungpa Rinpoche? She reads him. She likes Lama Tsultrim a lot, goes to Tara Mandala every week from Farmington. Took refuge with APR. We will dine on March 6 when she comes to ABQ for an acupuncture workshop. She has to go; she's got needles in a patient.

March 1

Dreams. "What is light?" Hint of APR.

Work. Old lady going to the doctor with a terminal illness. Om Ami Dewa Hri.

What is peak SLR? All the ice & snow on earth melted. When? How about peak GHG? Peak population? Peak food? Peak radiation?

I could call this book *Farewell to Florida—Meditations on Peak Everything*. I should get *Peak Everything* book.

March 2

"Reality is statements." From course I'm taking in dream. Dawa waits loyally outside.

Gas to $3.29. What will the peak oil price be? As usual, I'm talking long-term… I order *Peak Everything* by Richard Heinberg. Saw him on ecobuddhism.org.

Big Bang means we're all connected. The sandhill cranes. First I hear them, then see the winged flocks high in the azure sky, heading north. Mystery of time, Rio Grande, rainbow cloud. Later, from the cab: daffodils!

Gas $3.37. Ghaddafi bombs oil town. 71 degrees.

March 3

Dreamed I was kissing a made-up Nepali woman named "With You" —big ceremony amid tanks & soldiers.

Today is the last day of Tibetan year, a good day to clean away negativity. Dorje Trollo day. So I quickly dusted top of bookcase, cut my nails. To work. History happens. Hurting veteran. Poverty mentality. Rat race. Internal combustion.

Home to infected computer so they say. Unplug it. Lie down after dinner as usual. But get up to do protector prayer 21 times, AH, "Prayer for Extreme Times."

It may be magical thinking but it definitely changes the brain.

March 4

"The Teachings say that taking up the practices of the Four Immeasurables is essential for the attainment of liberation." —OR. They are immeasurable equanimity, love, compassion & joy. We should attempt to see that all sentient beings are equal in their wish to be happy & free of suffering. We should send forth the wish that they be happy (love) & free of suffering (compassion). "We should wish them 2 kinds of joy: joy in their worldly life, & also lasting joy, which is the attainment of liberation from suffering." These are the components of aspiration Bodhicitta, the wish that all attain enlightenment. Then there are the Paramitas, action Bodhicitta: giving, ethical discipline, patience, heroic effort, meditative concentration & wisdom. Hey, let's all become Bodhisattvas!

Longchenpa says that if compassion degrades into sentimentality, the antidote is joy. If joy falls into mere elation, the antidote is equanimity. If equanimity weakens into apathy, the counter to this is love. And if love becomes attachment, generate compassion. Longchenpa lived from 1308 to 1364 in Tibet.

The year of the Iron Rabbit. Coyote running at airport.

I finish *Penetrating Wisdom*. Great teacher, I bow to you, Dzogchen Ponlop Rinpoche.

March 5, Saturday

Guru dream—who was it?

I call my brother, Rick. He loves the earth, even poison oak. He is pulling it out since it's an invasive species in the San Francisco Bay area. He's part of a team working on that problem. He recently read *Eaarth* by Bill McKibben; I'll try to get it at the library. I mention peak value on the beach condo in Florida probably has passed. Love him. The true nature of mind never peaks...

After Nick fixes my computer infection, I go to the cab driver meeting. Worried about rising gas prices, the boss says go without AC.

No driver says anything but we are all thinking: are you kidding? In the desert summer? At least the idea of conservation is talked about.

Home to book in the mailbox, *Peak Everything* by Richard Heinberg, from Amazon. I look at a few graphs but I'm in no hurry to read about the century of decline...

I'm not driving out to Copper Mountain for the New Year practice & dinner. But at least I did some mantras.

March 6

I call Sue; it's her birthday. Brother Jon there; brief talk. Sue saw a female cardinal on her deck railing & thought it was Mom! Me: I think Mom did better than that...(birds have short, tough life & don't get the dharma). Jon excited about the spring training baseball game tomorrow (Rays).

Michael Moore: "400 Americans have more wealth than half of all Americans combined—America is NOT broke." Video of him speaking to the Wisconsin protesters. On Wisconsin!

"Missa Solemnis" by Beethoven. Then I do some extra driving so Ramona can come to our phowa practice. She says she can't afford the gas to go across town. We practice compassion & shooting our minds out the top of our heads. It sounds so crazy but OR says it works at the time of death & everybody in Tibet could do it. I give Ramona a CD; maybe she'll play it on the radio.

Home to blank messages. Nothing from R. I'm hyped to see her for dinner & it's 5:08. More Beethoven. Sad music here, reading about global warming refugees too. Agnus Dei. Could it be I'll be disappointed by R. again? Could be alright. Dona nobis pacem.

Baby! I wish you were sleeping with me tonight. She's so nice & pretty. Her acu-friend, Michelle, joined us for Japanese food. I worshipped R. but sometimes looked at Michelle to be polite. R., I have a question: why did you say you'd be my girlfriend once? She thinks she might have pneumonia again, is spending the night at Michelle's motel. Baby, two can live cheaper than one. I could love you to death...

March 7

Dream of lost boys, playing old guitar.

Love R. Wish her to be happy. Also compassion, rejoicing & equanimity. Send her an email. Also, call & leave message.

10:35 BAU. A no-go to start the cab day. $1441 per ounce: price of gold. AH.

Goodbye Florida—Meditations on Global Warming? Climate Catastrophe? Dust storm.

There is nobody like R. It's hard for me to get real.

March 8

Play. Start back of this notebook for *Goodbye Florida* ideas. Rejoice that R. is so nice & pretty. Rejoice for all the happily married people. Gas $3.49. Work & do Amitabha mantras. Pick up D. & her mom & mom's partner. She's been sick; had a surprise visit from her mom.

Run-off in NM is 75% of normal.

R., give me one good reason I can't love you…

March 9

Dream of smiling Ammachi, the hugging saint from India, another of my gurus. Her eyes see a child & me. Long dreams.

Knee not so good. Nothing from R. Kyrie eleison. Email her & call & leave message.

Cold wind; shelter of cab 447.

I'm trying to memorize the "Faithful Student Song" in Tibetan. The English version is a bit confusing. It's a spontaneous song by APR. Beautiful melody; great lyrics.

Great meaning. Here's the English: I ask precious three jewels, from deep in my pained heart, see me with compassion, I have no other hope. This dear human body, impermanence besets, will you be confident at death, good & faithful student? The 5 skandhas gather, & disperse who knows when, heartily think on death, good & faithful student. Karma never deceives, so give up harmful thoughts, strive in holy dharma, good & faithful student. This false swirl will deceive, mind free of attachment, long for liberation, good & faithful student. Your mind not two pointed, with unchanging faithful love, lama goes with loma, good & faithful student. Gyurme Thubten Gyatso, when heart holds him lama, there's no better guidance, keep heart talk in your heart. Ah ho a lala ho, pleasing play-song I offer, ah ho a lala ho, pleasing play-song I offer.

Chi is the Tibetan word for death.

Last fare of an irritable day is a non-violent communication seminar guy into zen teacher Okamura.

March 10

Peak coffee may be here due to climate change. The beans are very sensitive to heat & moisture. Peak chocolate next?

I work on dream song: this doesn't happen every day, to wake up with a dream in my head, a dream about a song in my head, a song about a dream. That's just about all I can say, I wake up & it's almost gone, I try to hold on but it's gone, a song about a dream. I don't remember who was there, I don't remember where we were, I just remember playing a song, a song about a dream. This life is like a dream they say, you wake up & it's almost gone, you try to hold on but it's gone, a song about a dream...

#46: when does it pick up, Bird?

Me: I don't know... (to myself: maybe we already peaked...)

Shannon calls! Got a job at a cafe & is training.

Work: a goddess & her lame-brain rich guy. He complains about the fare, lives in a mansion. I get a 47 cent tip. Watching her go in with him, I angrily say "good luck."

Do tonglen for Shannon, R., jerk, NPR, Libya. Dow down 208. No-fly zone for Libya? Beautiful sunset.

Shanny wrote down the 4 immeasurables & 6 paramitas to maybe use on her art designs.

March 11

"She Loves You" by the Beatles. Does she? "Get real" subverted by romanticism & biology.

Warm walk; see Angel the dog but knee hurts.

Fare: How hot does it get here in the summer?

Me: Well, our record is 107 but now we've got climate change...

Fare (scoffing): But you just had record cold!

11 am news: 8.9 earthquake in Japan. Plus tsunami...

1 pm news: nuclear reactor in Japan needs coolant —tsunami causes damage in Hawaii & CA.

Burning sun reminds me of summers past as I sit in the bullpen, wishing I was moving with the AC on. Then into shade of the staging area. Do I fear burning up? Tara, quick saviouress... Om tare tam soha.

Done for the week. Hallelujah! Listening to Beethoven's 4th symphony—natural beauty. Like R.

Saturday, March 12

Do I need magnesium again? Slept lightly, dreamed of a baby playing around my limp penis. New Dimensions radio: a car-free year by a guy from Whidby Island, Washington.

NYTimes: "Heaven is for Real." Three-year-old boy goes to heaven, finds that Jesus has blue eyes. "If Slaughterhouses Had Glass Walls," a video narrated by Sir Paul McCartney, on Facebook. I reshare.

Write Amber, re Cool Cabs. Go to eat at Pei Wei. Helped by a girl with a wonderful mouth. Read how to avoid peak food. It's a long shot.

Look at *Goodbye Florida* through tired eyes. It's too much like a diary.

5:30 news. JAPAN. Explosion at nuke; reactor meltdown possible. Grim search for survivors. Sea water being pumped into reactor. Second reactor problems too. Iodine pills ready. US west coast worries. Fascists in US Congress want to cut tsunami budget. Flooding in NE US.

March 13

Mountain Daylight Time. Bach cantata 182 on radio.

Go to Copper Mountain. A few of us rejoice, rest in mind-nature for a second or two. Come back home. Christine calls. She climbed Atalaya Peak today, alone, with no water. I say I'll take the train to Santa Fe next week. She inspires me to go for a walk in the neighborhood.

Tweets from Japan. The US should/shouldn't worry about radiation from there...

Guru yoga for all beings.

The quince bush is starting to bloom even though nobody's watered in a long time. Chris calls: he's watering his garlic.

5:30 news. 6 reactors in trouble; rolling blackouts to save electricity. Long lines for food, water & gas. Another quake could hit. Petrochemical plant burning. Obama still supports nukes.

Last week I was laughing with R.

Sue calls: our niece, Kelly had another baby; Jon went. I tell her, hesitantly, of my plan to take 3 months off. What do you do if you're an artist? A tired one, trying to save beings. I can't do it driving a cab. Or can I?

Song about a dream, new part.

Sue cares, doesn't want me to spend all my small inheritance. Will I wind up in Florida? Drowning in old age?

March 14

Off work today. But I have to go to Rio Rancho for shrink & counsellor. Woke in the dark with dream of playing music. Japan, misery on the radio.

Hike up Piedra Lisa rocks & contemplate city & world, do Kuntuzangpo prayer. Back down to notice I cut hand on rock. Warm now, knee good; looking forward to a hiking season!

Senator Bingaman defends nukes. Survivors in Japan bowing but not touching. Nukes too hot. Libyan rebels on the run. Wind blowing offshore in Japan, toward us.

Do Medicine Buddha practice. Can I go to bed at 7:30, 6:30 old time?

March 15

Neck hurts. Japan worse. Almost cry during preliminary practices.

Share "Driven to Tears" on FB. Police!

Headache in cab 448. Back in the uncomfortable saddle again. At least I'm somewhat useful; people need rides.

Willows leafing, forsythia blooming.

TH: global contamination. I breathe. Breathe in radioactivity, breathe out pure air. Tonglen. TH was in Germany during Chernobyl, says "nuclear power is insanity."

Starting to tire, I'm on the way to the VA. Reactor #4 waste is on fire; #2 containment breach.

March 16

Dream I'm writing, Preston, beneficent Dawa, an unknown animal for someone's pet.

73 days to go till my vacation; 37 days until OR is here. My brief fling with Dena was 2 years ago; Schubert is now.

TH: the nuclear waste is stored on the tops of the nukes. The power plants need the electrical grid to stay cool.

Sign says: Endless Seafood Buffet. Steak grilling smells like burning flesh (which it is). Hope fading in Libya. In Japan: hot waste. If they can get power on they can pump water over it.

March 17

Dream that I accidentally set on fire a pretty girl's blond hair. First night without my winter sleeping bag. 57 in the morning, going to 80.

Amitabha mantra at work: Om ami dewa hri.

1 pm Waiting for the hook. Cab wouldn't start after I picked up an old couple at retirement home. Nick, #58, came to rescue them. Walk while I wait to stretch old legs.

Back at the office, I decide to go home rather than taking out another cab. Get my drugs from sexy-as-hell Lilia from Guadalajara at Costco.

NPR at 5: UN votes for no-fly zone in Libya. In next 24 hours France could attack Ghaddafi's forces. Too late to save rebels? In Japan there are 1.6 million people without water.

March 18

Dream: "Bird W. Thompson, genius," an ad in a magazine. Who put it there? I'm embarrassed.

I buy a paper, our right-wing monopoly. *Albuquerque Journal*: "Part of State in Severe Drought." "January & February were 'one of the driest starts to a calendar year on record' according to Ed Polasko, hydrologist with the National Weather Service's Albuquerque office. Statewide precipitation since Oct. 1 is 56% of normal, and Albuquerque has gone 45 consecutive days without measurable precipitation... All eyes are now shifting to the summer monsoon season, which typically begins in early July, as offering the first clear chance for a respite... Meanwhile, the fire danger is rising. The state has seen 30 wildfires in the past week burn more than 5,000 acres…" (John Fleck).

All this is in line with the climate change models which the article fails to mention. Joe Romm (of *Climate Progress*) says to get out of the Southwest because of coming Dustbowl. But this is my home now. All nature is equal; take a stand wherever you are & fight GHGs…that's my motto. Stand till you have to move, that is. Then what?

Another new motto: I'd rather have rolling blackouts than radioactivity. Japan connection. Here we have Los Alamos, birthplace of the bombs which Truman dropped on Hiroshima & Nagasaki. Los Alamos has nuclear waste, tons of it.

Dispatcher says his wife likes my CD. At airport: Patricia, the security guard. She always has one song stuck in her head each day. The song today is "O Solo Mio." She asks if I have a song in my head. At the moment it's the Amitabha chant I say.

2:38, atomic weight of Uranium, poison

2:57, coyote at bullpen, limping

3, possible cease-fire in Libya

5, Fukushima now equal to Three Mile Island in terms of danger they say. Heroic efforts by nuclear workers.

March 19

Nightmare fight with Bob I think. Refugee in rain. Then I take acid at a lake; Rick & Sue & a crowd. VFW men in a raft; Colin Powell, John McCain country, peaks.

Lonely. Come here: University & Central, where anti-war march is assembling. I have a problem with sign that says "No War on Libya" but I guess I'll march anyway. There's also "Obama Kills" & "Free Bradley Manning" (the leaker to WikiLeaks). I'm for getting out of Afghanistan & Iraq but think Obama is trying. I try to talk to a guy about Libya: the rebels there were like us here protesting until they were attacked; what would we do if we were systematically shot down? He doesn't buy it.

We march downtown. But I skip the speeches thinking I can still get to the special Tara practice at Copper Mountain. But it's uphill to the car & I work up a sweat. I'm too late & too tired for the drive to Corrales so I go home & take a nap. Then do my own Tara full moon. I offer all the wishes for peace & all the beautiful girls I saw today to APR, OR & Ammachi. I bow to those beyond loneliness. Om tare tam soha. Om tare tutare ture soha.

I watch some basketball & then the super moonrise. AH.

March 20

Dream: get a cow. Is that like "get a horse"?

Voice mail from R.: she wasn't connected to the internet when she was moving her office. She says my complaint about her not connecting with me was too negative. Whatever. Too little, too late. Get real.

New song idea: I'm so lonely & you're so lovely. Let's get together some time?

I go to Copper Mountain. We do extra prayers for APR's birthday, full moon. Then to Santa Fe with the Mahavishnu Orchestra jamming. Soaring music. Christine here but has to leave; Chris is out walking the arroyo by St. John's College, his favorite walk. Paper says Santa Fe only grew by 9% in last decade. "Only"? Compared to what? NM grew 13%, to 2 million. ABQ bloated up 22%, to 546,000. Rio Rancho up 69%! Now it's 87,000. But who wants to live there?

I walk alone, down to the dry river. Walk the labyrinth too at Frenchy's Field, the one I helped make a little the day I got appendicitis. Om mani padme hung. See old friend, Drew, on the way back. He still smokes pot, is still with Charlene, feels bleak he says. He invites me to meat-eating BBQ some day & we exchange cards. I tell him I'm a vegetarian.

Chris comes home, tries out my super $100 meditation cushion which I'm not using because of my knee. I try out his chair cushion he had specially made. We trade. He's not so sure about Libya. Christine comes home; we eat enchiladas she made & play the game I brought with me, "Rebirth." It's an old Tibetan game with a die. Chris wins & gains enlightenment; I remain in the lower realms… A lot of fun with them. Next time: take the train. Bed at 10.

March 21

Up at 7:30. Not much time to practice. So tired. Work. Strong south wind; dust in the sky.

TH is against the UN support of Libyan rebels but Randi in favor.

Not one fare yet has asked me about the book on the dashboard, *Peak Everything*. Are people just not curious? Or are they in denial?

5:30, Brian is unloading the packed cab. I just brought him from a nice townhome to funky Nendel's Motel. With his dog. He has a brain injury —hit with a baseball bat as he was sleeping in the street in LA. He also said he was enlightened but he was sure stressed out by the sudden move. Fortunately, his case worker was waiting at the motel to help him. So young.

March 22

Kiss dream. Empty emptiness —bodhi svaha.

"Wind power surged from 17,000 megawatts to 194,000 MW in past decade." *Climate Progress*. New title for book: *Everything Disappears — A Buddhist's View of Global Warming Etc*. Emphasize the positive sometimes? What to do when everything disappears—even "you"? Rest in the true nature of awareness, don't grasp. Everyone you see is a dead person. Dead before; dead again. Collective karma too. Mass markets, mass production, mass media, the masses. Population boomed with cheap oil. Now what? Crash; mass die-offs.

Randi plays Kucinich saying to impeach Obama. George W. Bush let Ghaddafi keep his mustard gas, claimed he was a pal for not pursuing nukes. An oil pal.

Work on new song: turning loneliness into loveliness...

O Trish! You are a goddess! She is new in office; I say we should go for a hike sometime. O Gloria! You are a saint! She works at the gas station where drivers now fill up. She's from Mexico not Iraq as I first guessed.

March 23

Dream: Christmas with my family of origin.

My back hurts & body. Walk anyway. Work anyway? Crammed in a cab all day? Call in sick, go back to bed.

The spring winds are wild this year. Today my eyes burn & the view of the mountains is obscured by dust (& pollen). Positive ions are bad for you, I've heard. We need some negative ions, some rain, sweet rain. Former tenants I guess didn't water the sycamore tree. It died. Then I didn't water the spruce enough & it died. The trees in the city are great but it's a job keeping them hydrated. Prayer flags blow, spreading good energy to the earth & beyond. A no-car day.

OR: wave & ocean the same thing. Thought & mind. Or no-mind. Audio from website brings me his musical voice of sanity.

Beauty Elizabeth Taylor dead at 79. Iodine 131 in Tokyo water.

Mozart.

Chapter 3
OR

March 24

Wake at 4 & get up. Devotion in the dark. For the Buddha-nature shining from APR, OR...me & you...

Too much news. Reminder that we live in a degenerate time. Maybe it can inspire compassion, action. Music is a good alternative.

Work. By noon I am definitely not getting rich. Thinking about Florida. How much would siblings charge me for rent at a beach condo? As Rick says, I could watch the tide get higher (he'll give me a shovel)...Or maybe I should move to CO to be close to OR. Or maybe stay here & keep working.

Wind. Sixth day of coalition air-strikes on Libya. Oil is $105 per barrel. Randi says Ghaddafi has an all-female security detail of 40 virgins.

Democracy Now. Japanese dead or missing is 26,000. 15 dead in Syrian protests. TEPCO tries to fix Fukushima. I pick up 4 Baptists with smart phones. They are Bible translators. Think to myself, what do they know of Buddha-nature?

I gas up & find that Gloria smokes. At office, I learn that Trish is changing back to her maiden name. She is so sexy.

At home. Sue calls; she's better after being sick. Florida v. BYU. She cheers for her alma mater; I cheer for the western basketball team.

March 25

I am blue. Play music anyway. No time before work though.

"Imagine" by John Lennon is one of my favorite songs. But I think it's actually good to imagine a heaven & a hell. The Tibetan teachings do. Without a resultant suffering for negative actions, there would be no cause & effect. Likewise, for positive actions there are positive results. To imagine a heaven doesn't take away from enjoyment of the moment. To imagine a hell might cause fewer negative actions. But Lennon was looking at things as a rebel against Christianity's solidified ideas.

The Buddha taught that everything is impermanent & changing, even heaven & hell realms. The Christian concept of eternity without change doesn't seem based in reality. Imagining dying is also important—

because it's going to happen. Otherwise, there is denial. I also try to imagine the after death states which OR writes about. And that this world is a pure land. It is pure from the quark's point of view, from the Big Bang point of view. An amazing display of energy & light & beings & awareness. And the Tibetan meditation of visualizing oneself as a deity of wisdom & compassion can bring one realization of egolessness, the true state of mind. A few thoughts while I wait for a fare at the airport.

March 26, Saturday

Wake with a start. KUNM: a Rumi devotee says to become plural. I'm glad I'm a Buddhist. Light comes into the room. I get up & light a candle & incense. Do my morning practice.

After breakfast, I get an old box for candles & label it "Death Box—Open if Bird is Dying." I start writing a sort of a dharma will as OR suggests. It's pretty simple but at least I started. My dharma vision is to complete the *ngondro* guru yoga from APR & his secret oral instructions. But my will's first item is to contact Helen so she can contact OR. Hopefully, he could do phowa for me.

Work on new song a while, "Turning Loneliness into Loveliness." Inspired by daffodils!

After lunch, I drive east & hike to Travertine Falls. Drought in the desert but here it's a miracle of water. It's on the surface for 20 yards, falls over the limestone ledge & is gone back into the ground in another 20 yards. My heart beats fast from the climb & then rests again. Once I heard a canyon wren here. Sandia Mountains.

Back into the city, doing Vajrasattva mantras to purify my use of gas. Was it worth it? Via Whole Foods for pizza & smiles of girls. Home for Sweet 16. I call Chris. Old friend Larry answers. He & his daughter, Aurora, came over from AZ. She might have a job in Los Lunas.

A news-free day, almost.

March 27

I ride with Helen to Eldorado for a phowa get-together. Find I've been doing part of the visualization wrong. Still learning the practice. First, the senses dissolve; then the elements & the outer breath stops. That's when the bardo of life ends & the bardo of dying begins. Where will I be then? In a hospital, at home, drowning in a hurricane? Will I remember mindfulness & awareness?

Lunch with David & Louise.

Home to a call from Preston. Florida has just passed a law hurting unions. He might visit me in summer.

March 28

Day off.

Take my car to Jim's Auto. Major work. It won't be ready until tomorrow. I decide to walk home with daffodil song working in my head. An hour walk; good for me, knee OK. When I get back, I offer lilacs to precious lama.

Radio: Obama to speak tonight on Libya. Three types of plutonium in soil near Fukushima. Half a million people protest austerity cuts by UK conservatives. There is a US Uncut too.

I call Rick. He just spent a week in Death Valley; the spring flowers were good. He saw a black-chinned sparrow. He says I should look into senior housing. Don't want to hear it.

I work on song. Work on "High & Dry," chapter 2 of whatever this book is called.

There are daffodils again, sunny daffodils in the wind, turning loneliness into loveliness. I've been wasting so much time, instead of opening my mind & turning loneliness into loveliness. Do you know what I'm saying, do you hear what I'm playing? I've been lonely for a while, it's so good to see you smile, turning loneliness into loveliness...

Obama speaks; I think it's a good speech. Ghaddafi has got to go.

Lie down & listen to Shostakovitch First Symphony. Wow.

March 29

Dreams. Twenty years of gold left: reality.

Take cab to work. And from work to Jim's Auto. $1496 for my 97 Toyota Camry. I hope it lasts a long time. It gets 28 mpg but will that be enough?

Via Whole Foods home. Marie, you drive me crazy.

March 30

Shannon calls. She's going to Tucson with Aaron & Lynn for a big craft show. But first, to judge for a ticket, to work & a Ram Dass thing. Busy. I send her some money.

Give a CD to a girl named Mel who works in uranium clean-up. Class of 05 Sandia High; same as Shannon. Also recommend *Peak Everything* to her. Then a DOE woman who thinks nukes are safe. Educate her about uranium mining & waste in our nuclear state. I show her the Heinberg book too; peak uranium not that far off.

Radio: Ed Schultz says to arm the Libyan freedom fighters.

March 31

Dream of gators.

Meltdown in Japan. 130,000 more to evacuate; 70,000 already displaced.

I go to the eternal recurrence of the taxi life.

22 days until OR is here.

I finish *Peak Everything*. No mention of possibility of enlightenment or bodhisattvas. Secular. It took me 26 days to read during breaks in driving. Plenty of time to finish today. The book wasn't political enough either. The Republicans are pro-Big Oil & Big Coal. Anti-science. Come right out & say it, Heinberg.

Tom Root tells dispatcher he's on Cherry St. but I see him on Maple. Booze-addled brain. He's on a round trip to buy more alcohol.

April 1

Dream of Chenrezi practice, apple grower John Brownfield. Venus & crescent moon in dawn light. What a beautiful world!

In cab, waiting for Dori & son. Boy, is it hot! Head for shade. BAU for me—comforting but stifling. Dori does astrology, says I need my freedom, being an Aries. "Though the Masters make the rules, for the wise men & the fools, I've got nothin Ma, to live up to…"

The daffodils are fading. I ask Evangeline out. She'll think about it. She's from the Phillipines, in ABQ for fun she says. I give her my card. Hopeless.

A text from Shannon at the Tucson crafts show. She says she just met Don Henley! I start thinking how I can get my CD to him. But then she admits it was an April Fool's joke. I text back that I just picked up J.Lo.

Beautiful women everywhere!

49

Democracy Now. Jim Messina is Obama 2012 campaign manager. Big donors to raise a billion dollars. Yemen protests, Egypt, Syria.

At gas station I find that Gloria has a boyfriend. She has such a nice smile & Mexican accent.

Saturday, April 2

White lilacs. But so dry. Nobody moved here thinking about running out of water. I know I didn't.

Nick comes over; we record 3 songs & do other things. My voice is always iffy these days.

A trip to Whole Foods, intestinal trouble, lonely basketball. Phowa!

April 3

I wake at 3 with a headache. Get back to sleep.

Dzigar Kongtrul Rinpoche link from FB. He says guilt needs to be confessed & purified. I never thought guilt was so bad but now I see it is. Om benzra sato hung. Ego is confusion.

Call sister. They had 5 inches of rain in Terra Ceia & a tornado near Sue's office in Pinellas County. Her friend, Carol, is getting chemo but her cancer might be terminal. I always wanted to talk to Carol but never got the chance...

I complete 3,000 Guru Rinpoche mantras today. In time for ABC News: sexual harassment in college, rip in jet roof at 36,000 feet, BP to get new drilling permits in Gulf of Mexico? Local news: fire near Ruidoso. Another very windy day; my eyes burn.

April 4

Wake at 3:30 & can't get back to sleep.

8:47, 36 degrees, predicted high is 65. I have time to play "Revolution," "While My Guitar Gently Weeps," "One Earth, One Sky." But have to go to work. I will try to see work as bodhicitta today.

Driving, I do get a sense of accomplishment & self-esteem & sociability. Different than being alone, meditating or writing. OR says worldly & dharma are different. Ultimately the same, but not now.

A list of my fares today: 1. Mohammed Nur ("light"), young Ethiopian who works at the nursing home, 2. still waiting for #2 at 12:16

at airport—it's a beauty, going to Pueblo Cultural Center, 3. woman into green Vancouver, BC, 4. pre-school worker, 15 cent tip, 5. businessman talking on his cell about $170,000 salary, 6. Cheryl & Beth, the blind partners going to the Y to exercise, 7. a black woman from the VA, 8. another black woman from the gay club, drunk. That's it, for 8 hours & now I'm really tired.

But Bob in office is talking to drivers about saving gas (it's up to $3.64 today). He says the management is freaking out over energy costs. I say they should have seen it coming & bought hybrids. Anyway, there will be a driver meeting on April 23, when OR is in town. I start thinking of gas-saving ideas…

Home: LeeAnn Rimes sings of bombs bursting in air & it's Butler vs. UConn. The Huskies win the NCAA championship.

April 5

10:15, dragged myself to work. Actually, cab-driving is a pretty solitary life too. I call D. & leave message. Boredom at airport. Try to practice the 4 immeasurables; read a little. A salmon expert who asks about OR's book. We have a good conversation. Maybe she'll read it.

Bad day for making money. But I've learned the "Faithful Student Song" in Tibetan.

Radio: nukes in densely populated India a bad idea. Nukes all over the earth a bad idea.

Serenity, a beautiful 14-year-old, with her mom. I've got a one track mind sometimes. Until guru yoga.

April 6

Gabrielle! Out watering her yard near my house. I say I've always liked her bumperstickers on her Prius: Choose Joy!, Be Amazing! She wants to talk: single mom, age 40, says her weight goes up & down, into snow-boarding, kayaking, has a 17-year-old son. I say I'm not that athletic anymore. She plays music too. I'll drop by my card & CD after work.

Then first fare is a blond, Vegas babe & her rich guy, meeting for 3 day tryst here. Kisses in the back seat. She talks about shoes, clothes, nipples! Second fare is Pavan, the new sound engineer for Linda Perry & Deep Dark Robot. I give him a CD.

51

Noon, NPR: government shut-down looms. Dems blame Repubs blame Dems. Oil at $109; gas, $3.71.

A crazy pot-head vet on medical marijuana.

Jeff, mellow vet with MS, also smokes dope. He says I could teach Gabrielle about Buddhism. She went snow-boarding 20 times this last winter...

Randi: Google doesn't pay any taxes, or Rupert Murdoch. Corporate loopholes.

Don't get attached I tell myself. But I'm attached. After work, give Gabrielle my CD; she's on FB.

Safe at home. Chris Rawlins calls. He still thinks he can heal himself from diabetes with mantras. Good long talk.

April 7

A sprinkle of rain! I sleep through news till 7:30.

If Gabrielle was 27 years older than me, she'd be 94. *NYTimes*: new particle? new force? a proton weighs one billion electron volts. What is beyond existence & non-existence I wonder. Beyond attachment & non-attachment... Rain in the bullpen.

Noon: aftershock in Japan at 7.1. Slow day in cab; at least I'm not polluting. Then I go to Moriarty with a part for trucker Pablo. He's happy to see me.

Buddha Lives! Buddha Saves! Buddha is the Way! Real Men Love Buddha! Buddha Died for Your Sins! Buddha Loves You! I make $103 in 9 hours.

Home to Gabrielle on FB. She has lots of friends. Get real.

April 8

Day off. It's Dad's death day. 1997. His body was so agitated from his blood disease: hiccups without end. He endured it without a word. I finally asked the hospice nurse for something to calm him down. And then he died. I had told him he would go through different dreams after death. But I had trouble talking about what I believed. What did he believe? He never talked about it to me. Anyway, he's reborn somewhere now, a good rebirth I'm sure.

Remembering Marie too, from the store. Such a nice person, with such nice skin. I message Gabrielle that I'd like to have dinner with her.

Skip a haircut, go to library. Put a hold on *Eaarth*, get DVD of *Portrait of the Artist as a Young Man*. I feel drained.

NPR: fierce fighting in Misrata, Libya. Oil $113. Japanese in the dark. Computers in schools; no need for books or paper!

Chris calls back: he's busy tomorrow—no train ride to Santa Fe for me. We look at the young moon. Later. Loud robins at sunset. I watch *Portrait*. Serious artist, not as jokey as the real James Joyce. My guts hurt.

Saturday, April 9

I walk in the wind. Infusion of lilac fragrance. Government shutdown averted.

But CO_2 level is at 392.40 for March. It's the highest March in 2 million years...

Call Rick; finish taxes with his advice.

52 mph gusts here. Guru, my eyes burn. Hey, I could have a car-free day. I lie down with Tara mantras. Fast for lunch. Can't see the peak for the dust in the wind. Lora Lucero on FB is sick; I will do Medicine Buddha for her & myself. Call Norma later.

April 10

I need the gas heat this morning. Imagine rainbow light.

American Forests intend to plant 100 million trees by 2020.

Richard Dawkins video from Mike Peters on FB. It's very good militant atheism. Second most popular choice in a poll was "non-religious" (after Christian). But, as most atheists, Dawkins doesn't take into account a non-theistic religion such as Buddhism. Which offers the tools for great personal transformation, even enlightenment. May the precious Bodhicitta arise where it has not arisen, i.e. may all beings attain enlightenment.

I pick up Ramona & we go to phowa practice & video talk by OR. Helen gives me a little Chenrezi statue for my birthday. Great talk.

Then to Foods. I give Marie my card. She's so cool: she says I must be a real rockstar to be so low profile. I love her glasses, her sassy chassis, that she's not on-line, her mystery.

Good story on climateprogress email about drought in the Southwest.

Sue reports headaches. Whipporwill calling from the swamp.

April 11

"The soul of sweet delight can never be defiled"—William Blake

Didn't sleep well. OR talk lingers in my mind. I put his photo up higher on my altar beside APR. Non-dual lamas.

I get a small check for 8 days work minus $60 for their overpay on last check & 2 charged cab rides when my car was in the shop.

Terrible blue sky. So many songs like "Blue Skies smiling at me…" but those songs weren't written in the desert.

I dreamed of the Santa Fe stupa area again; Lama Dorje had a weird little pet.

Western kingbirds playing chase near the bullpen. Are they mating? They sing a little.

Home to FB: Gabrielle says she's too busy for dinner but she liked my CD, especially "Ah—The Perfection of Wisdom in One Syllable." I'm lonely & anxious until I do some guru yoga.

April 12

Nightmare of ego, power, sex, drugs & over-population. I couldn't find my car to get away from it all. I wake with a dry mouth.

It's my BIRTHDAY! (It's your birthday too). Put on the Beatles. I was born in a small hospital in Cornplanter's Kingdom (NW Pennsylvania). I loved my Mommy & feared my Daddy. But my Daddy sang…& made me laugh…

Rick, loving brother, sends me a $20 save the wolf stamp, a card, his photo of pelicans flying in the sunset & a check for $200!

I go to work. TH says Wikipedia etc. being attacked by billionaires paying internet activists to spin things their way. I sing my song "Money to Burn," a little angry. Cotton price up 15%; oil down. Shanny calls! She's so sweet to me, says she's glad I was born. Chris calls! Zen talk: everything was born the day I was born…I say "form is emptiness." When does joy become elation? Equanimity needed.

Checking out at office window with Trish, I comment on her pretty hair. Then I ask her if she heard me when I said we should hike sometime. Trish: yes, I said that would be fun. Oh, she turns me on—what a beautiful face! I get her number & give her a card. Then Adrianna asks why she didn't get a card...I give her one & head for Whole Foods. Marie not there. She's probably 25 at most; Trish, 45? Me, 67.

Home to calls from siblings minus Bob, plus Christine. Then I can't settle down to sleep, attached to Trish's hair & face...

April 13

Mom's birthday.

A fare with a Nuk Detector gadget. He flies cargo to Tokyo.

Obama speaks: tax the rich & cut spending too. Amanda, new security guard at airport, sees my *Guru Yoga* book & introduces herself as a Buddhist too. No time to talk though. A fare says it was 100 degrees in Phoenix on April 1.

Trish says early afternoon is a good time to call. Home to box of cookies & a book on birding from Sue. Also, a card from Bob. Climate progress; 1000 mantras.

April 14

Three women on my mind; mind itself, empty. "Kiss the joy as it flies."

A windy day. I'm waiting at the 7-11 for a young Indian who only has a $100 bill. He's getting brew so he doesn't feel his upcoming tattooing so bad. He's from Jemez. His mom does pottery so he's getting one of her designs on his calf.

12:08, call Trish & leave a message. Sweet voice.

Dust in the air, gusts. Gusts lift dust; I can smell it. Pick up Dori & David at Walmart. She gets into talking about how Jefferson was a Rosicrucian. I doubt it but she insists. After we unload the groceries, she shows me a statue of Ramses in her glass cabinet. He is on his chariot. I thought he was just another big-shot Pharaoh but to Dori he's some kind of wise being.

5:45, going in, hoping to see Trish. Yes, she checks me out; says she got my message but was already at work, answering phones. She has the most kissable lips, the sweetest personality. She lives in Rio Rancho near trails & has a big yard for her 4 dogs. A son who survived Iraq.

Climate Progress: Clean energy program lives on; Bloomberg, Clinton join forces to fight climate change—Malibu Lagoon restoration controversy: Science wins (for now)—Should we really be encouraging

55

the export of American coal to China?—Budget compromise protects air pollution safeguards, Big Oil benefits are spared—Obama calls for more energy investments while proposing to cut deficit $4 trillion, slams GOP for a 'vision of our future that's deeply pessimistic' —Flashback: Donald Trump & his hair join the climate zombies—Bolivia: where adaptation equals abandonment—The contango game: how Koch Industries manipulates the oil market for profit.

April 15

Incredible String Band sweetness from YouTube. What is it to love someone? Every day? And if she's a Republican or closed-minded? We shall see. Maybe I could teach her. Did I ever have healthy attachment? Mom? Can I love myself? She's probably a Democrat, being a Gonzales. Is she Catholic? Only one child…

She calls on the way to work. She can't hike on Sunday because she has to do her taxes. She has family in Santa Fe & here, Easter coming…OK, bye.

The Life of the Skies by Jonathan Rosen. The author has "intellectual anxieties" about evolution. Loves birds though.

So much coming up about Mom & Dad, Oedipus, three poisons, love, sex. The poisons are the negative emotions of anger, attachment & ignorance. How about lunch tomorrow, Trishy Wishy?

There's a Tea Party rally at Menaul & Louisiana: Cut Taxes, etc. Deluded tools of the ruling class, Koch Brothers. It's big…

Trish says she'll meet me tomorrow for lunch at PF Chang's. Hope & fear, anyone?

April 16, Saturday

I wake at 4:30 with a clear dream of Rainbow Gathering in the woods somewhere. I'm offered grass but I pass. I help raise a big tent, saying "I've been to gatherings before but I'm new at this one."

Get up & do it. Walk around block at sunrise.

T. minus one hour. My usual Saturday irritable bowel syndrome. Shit!

After a little hug, Trish drives off in her black Mustang with an Oakland Raiders shield sticker on it (she's been a fan for 31 years). She is off to the cab office. Well, she's a non-practicing Catholic, she liked

56

Michael Moore's *Fahrenheit 9/11* which she saw with her son who lives with her, hoping to become a cop. She looked chubbier than I could see through the thick window at the office. Oh, we come from 2 different worlds, Trish. I gave her my CD; she offered the hug. Nice. I am into sports somewhat, right?

Home to buy *Gas Hole* documentary DVD on-line. ABC News: gas headed for record high price (the record average price was $4.11 in July 2008). Japan's ghost towns. 141 tornadoes in the South, 25 dead. Softball-sized hail.

April 17

Dream of a woman who could make her 2 eyes into 1!

I'm skipping Copper Mountain & going to Earth Day event at the Food Coop.

Meet Elke Duerr there. She is making a film about wolves. I think about getting a booth at the street fair next year for my CD(s) & book. The flamenco dancers are good; angels dancing. A Japan support group; lots of plants for sale. Then a guy with a vegan T-shirt with lots of reasons to be vegan. He gives me his card: Plant Peace Daily, JC Corcoran. I come home & go to his website. Good, ethical argument for veganism on a video there. I've been a vegetarian for 3 years. I had a dream in which a monastery full of monks moved aside to let a spider go out unharmed. Was APR in that dream? He advocates vegetarianism for his students. And brother Rick has been a vegetarian for many years. The last thing I gave up was fish oil which I figured I needed for my bipolar brain cells. I felt the same without it. Now I'm thinking about the extra water & grain needed for dairy & eggs. And how humans are short on water & grain. And how much more greenhouse gases are produced from dairy & eggs. And how the male chickens & cattle somehow aren't accounted for. So tomorrow I'll have a vegan day.

It's 82 degrees, 11 above normal. Humidity 9%; happiness 90%(?) Full moon, Palm Sunday.

News: 45 deaths in 6 states—243 tornadoes in 12 states in 3 days—April average is 150. Boehner in Iraq; radioactive fish off Japan.

YouTube: Smedley Butler & the American Liberty League. Corporate fat cats wanted the general to oust FDR but Smedley smelled a rat. JPMorgan, DuPont etc still at it with Tea Party ideas. Supreme Court

& the House of Representatives taken over by corporatists. OK, I'll call them fascists again, heartless fascists…

April 18

Dream I squish a tiny white bug with my thumb. Santa Fe river is raging & someone falls in. An Indian cave. Dreams.

Go to see Jon, my counsellor. Good session. Then praise for Pilar, new woman at check-out from the clinic, with no rings on. I have rings around my eyes though. Maybe next time I'll talk to her more. But I have to work.

A million acres of TX burned in last 12 days. I drive a guy from airport to movie studio on Mesa del Sol. Bulldozers out there: a city of 60,000 is planned in the desert dust. It was held back by the recession/depression but now is a go. Where will they get the water? The developers are running on momentum from the days of ignorance & cheap oil. We need a culture shift at every level; but the media is running on the same fumes as other corporations…Peak oil per capita passed long ago…

Bullpen: a gust blows away my copy of "Entering the City of Omniscience" but I chase it down.

Leave a message for Trish. She didn't know the difference between a Buddhist & a Muslim. Sweetness. Completeness. I am like a mute eating honey; I can't tell you what it's like… Honey, much sweeter than money, I am yours… Words & music come together… Nectar, nectar from the vector…

Japan to see radiation for months. BP blow-out anniversary coming. *Black Tide* author Antonia Juhasz on *D.Now*. Two million gallons of dispersant. Deep-water drilling too high tech, not understood but used anyway by the oil giants… BP still owes $20 billion.

5:37, no callback. Baby, please don't tell me maybe, I am yours if you call me, yeah all of me, is yours…

Done for the day, I figure out my cab mpg: 21.2. Better than I thought it would be.

No callback. No writing in the evening; too tired & uninspired usually after driving 8 hours.

April 19

Wake at 4:30. So much arises in my mind: old songs, people, desire, fear, ideas…

French toast for breakfast. But what about the chickens? Coming soon: a vegan week. But I've got yogurt & eggs I don't want to waste. Walk & see first roses, ants, the thrasher. Then try chords to "Sweetness" or "Yours." EmAD, G… Have to go to work.

Airport, sitting behind big Tony in the Yellow Cab. "Sweetness" herself hasn't called yet. Or is sweetness the sparrows hopping by the curb?

TH: Ayn Rand was a sociopath; Greenspan was a cult member who called others "parasites."

26 days of work after today. I make a little calendar in my notebook. #58, Nick, comes over to bullshit in the bullpen. I wonder what disease he has to talk like he's drunk & walk funny.

Next fare is a corporate attorney, talking on his cell. He's excited that Billy Tauzin is on board with one of his deals. Tauzin was the US Senator I think who helped Big Pharma on the Medicare bill of Bush & then went through the revolving door to be a drug lobbyist. Did these guys learn anything in Sunday school? He keeps talking; I start tonglen for Tauzin, Shanny, Mom, Dad, Trish, Ayn Rand…

Lots of time later to read *Life of the Skies*—Walt Whitman, Thoreau.

Trish is in the office but she doesn't check me out. I let it go.

On FB I find Bill McKibben's fiery speech to 10,000 youth at Power Shift 2011 in Washington DC. He reminds us that last summer it hit a world record 129 degrees in Pakistan & then a third of the country was flooded by the Indus River. And in this country the US Chamber of Commerce is allied with fossil fuels to fight the EPA.

April 20

Dream that Shannon & I are on top of a giant stupa. Also, a millet restaurant with death food.

FB: Maxim's UFO share. Amazing clips from local news around the world. Will there shortly be an announcement from the government? Maxim (Karma Samten) says the Tibetans call UFOs "za." Do not fear the za I say…

The Vajrayana vehicle is fast they say. Tibetan Buddhism. One can get enlightened in this lifetime...

I could make more money selling CDs on the street. But there is time to write. TH: 5 corporations run the media, ignore Power Shift. There were 22 arrests for civil disobedience. Risingtide.org. TX: burning from border to border. AK: governor is former Conoco-Philips lobbyist. Libya: Oscar- nominated photographer is killed.

Honey, you make my days so sunny, I am yours alone, come home, I'm yours. She called back briefly saying she was so busy at 2 jobs & not allowed to use phone... Yours like the stars & the moon & the sun, woman I want to be yours... I was once asked about R.: is she yours?

Two days to OR.

April 21

Helen says a woman wants to stay with me for the teachings. Great! I have a vacant Shanny room I volunteered.

It's going to be a long, hot summer. Long. Hot. There are about 1,000 houses in my neighborhood. I figure this out from counting houses per block & then looking on the map. It's called Bel Air. Working class.

TH has the director of *Gas Hole* on. First diesel was run on peanut oil. That's about all I hear before a customer needs a ride.

Angel, I like your arrangement, I am yours, be mine, be kind, & you'll find I'm yours...

April 22

I fear the za & evil, unknown. But bodhicitta prevails.

I have scheduled this day off so I can be ready for OR (& I'm sick of work).

Earth Day officially. *NYTimes* "As Consumers Cut Spending, 'Green' Products Lose Allure." FB: Akilah speaking on climate change with a clip from Alec Loorz, founder of kids against global warming. Alright!

Give myself some time to work on songwriting. Yours like the clouds & the rain & the trees, girl don't you see I am yours... Edit that part out & print it. By 10 am, my get up & go has got up & went. But I do more guru yoga, clean house a bit, go get bipolar drugs.

CP: Chesapeake suspends fracking in PA after blowout & leak.

Google has put more than $350 million into clean power.

Top 3, all GHG emissions:

1. China 16.4%
2. US 15.7%
3. Brazil 6.5%

TX Gov. Rick Perry officially proclaims 3 "days of prayer for rain"—starting on Earth Day.

YouTube: "peak oil strikes 2012–2015—oil price spike causes Worldwide Depression & Food Shortages." Could happen. US oil production peak was 1970; Canada, 74, UK-North Sea, 99. In 2005, 33 countries were past peak production. "World Map of Peak Oil Production."

"Dust of the rivers does murmur & weep…"

6:15, All set up at Sawmill Lofts for OR & his wife & translator, Melissa. Michael is off to get them at the airport; it's a short flight from Denver. Helen & I here, waiting for action. It's a nice rotunda, at Ramona's housing complex in Old Town. Attendance 14. I sit on couch beside Maxx, grasping (not literally). She's a haircutter, gave me her card. She usually goes to RigDzin Dharma Center.

Rinpoche has grown his black moustache & goatee. He could be Jigme Lingpa for all I know. He is Tibetan & has only been here 5 years but speaks good English. He prefers Tibetan for accuracy in his teaching most of the time. We bow to him, touching our foreheads to the floor three times…

Tonight it's phowa instruction & practice. Rinpoche teaches like it's the first time, with animation & enthusiasm. What we want is freedom from fear & doubt he says. We need faith & devotion & bodhicitta. Our minds are blindly blown about by the winds of karma. We need to steady the mind through the visualization. It's all in the book, but there's nothing like hearing it straight from the lama's mouth… He teaches, then we practice together. Wonderful! He says phowa is like a lifeguard: unless you can swim, you can't save others…

The woman who was going to stay with me didn't show up.

April 23

I get my private interview with Rinpoche before the day's teachings begin. I ask about my endless girl-search. He says don't try so hard & something might happen. "Best partner is dharma." He says that he & APR are really one, same lineage. I tell him of my up-coming time off & writing & going to CO. He asks if I can afford the time off. My answer is yes & no. Yes, in the short run; no, in the long run. He praises me, says book is a good idea. He tells me to get organized.

He teaches on Longchenpa's last words. He was told by Tibetan masters that this text is important for Westerners. It hasn't been translated into English yet. Longchenpa gave this teaching to benefit Buddhists in the future.

Couldn't work without translators such as Vairotsana & Melissa. A great pandita went to Tibet once from India but there were no translators where he went. He became a shepherd & never taught.

When Melissa is translating, often Rinpoche meditates. His face changes; he looks like he's in total awe. When he speaks, it is musical almost.

"Your worldly work mostly increases your afflictions. The deception of samsara increases. How to alleviate mental suffering? Not through worldly activity or self-deceptive wisdom but through seeing things as impermanent & lessening attachment. We need a balance between worldly & dharma. Make space to practice. Have compassion for yourself."

That was a paraphrase of course. Forgive me, Rinpoche & Melissa. How much of the teachings should I write here?

He says a lama is a guide through a fearsome land. One needs a deep, mature relationship with a lama. Long-term. With patience on both sides, minds will come together.

I talk with David Bacon, another eco-buddhist, about an interview for book. He says I should talk to Cynthia Jurs too, about her earth-treasure vases which she is burying around the world. David says Midland TX is almost out of H2O. Where will they all go? Maxx spins her prayer wheel. She's so friendly.

Home to find *Gas Hole* in the mailbox. But first, news. More tornadoes, caused by La Nina they say. Price at the pump? Obama says clean energy is the only solution. Then comes *The Ten Commandments* starring Fraser Heston as the infant Moses & Charlton Heston as the adult Moses. It's from 1956, Cecil B. DeMille. "And man was given dominion" & he dominated himself too. I watch from ancient Egypt to the Hyundai Santa Fe commercial & turn it off."

Shell Oil was 5 cents a gallon once. Tom Ogle got 100 mpg with his "vapor engine" once & then was found dead. Oil companies keep supply low says *Gas Hole*: no new refineries in the US in 30 years. Congressional hearings are chaired by politicians who take from Big Oil, such as Joe Barton (R-TX). Since 1990, Big Oil has given $49 million to Dems; $150 m to Repubs. When George W. Bush took office in January, 2001, gasoline was $1.47 a gallon. In May, 2007, it was $3.12. And now we have peak oil upon us.

Pretty good DVD. Time for bed.

April 24

Part of my *ngondro* is *"lama khyen"* (know me). Know me, Rinpoche! I cry.

It's Easter. *The Messiah* is on KHFM: "O death, where is thy sting?" Rest in peace is like rest in the true nature of awareness.

Maxx brings her son, 14, to see OR. Another hug.

The kindness of all beings, who have been our mothers in past lives—listen to the teachings for them. Rinpoche is cool, calm & collected, as usual. How does Melissa get all this in her notes for translating? Let your body be like a mountain, your mind like an ocean...

Louise asks how Atiyoga relates to suffering beings. OR: renunciation is compassionate; don't be depressed by the immense suffering. Results of meditation will be a decrease in self-attachment & an increase in love & compassion. We should make great effort before our elements go out of balance. Don't be discouraged. We will see others die & then we will die: be prepared.

Longchenpa tells his students to pray to him.

And then they are gone, back to Denver. I help clean up before going to Whole Foods. I give adorable Marie a CD at last & she promises to listen to it.

CP: "The American pika, a mountain-dwelling mammal in the West, does not do well in temperatures above 78 degrees —4 of 10 local pika extinctions have occurred since 1999..." They are so cute with their little round ears; I've seen them in the high country, among the rocks. Others will die...

CP: "Under pressure from industry, Congressional Republicans are urging the US EPA to further delay long-overdue rules that would limit more than 80 air toxics emitted by coal-burning power plants, barely a month after the agency announced them. According to the EPA, the mercury & air toxics standards alone would prevent up to 17,000 premature deaths & 11,000 heart attacks each year."

Bob calls. He's with Rick & Sue at the beach. They saw lots of birds, including a barred owl which attacked a bald-headed man. Hello to everyone; Happy Easter!

CP: Polar ice sheet mass is speeding up, on pace for one foot SLR by 2050. We are at a climate tipping point that, once crossed, enables multi-meter SLR this century.

I call Shanny. She's with her mom & half-siblings in Albuquerque. Her sister brought her down from Taos but can't take her back. As usual on a holiday, Shannon is overwhelmed by short time & lots of people to see. I want to see her but...

Chapter 4
What Do Buddhists Do?

April 25

A Monday-like feeling; back to work. Daughter called to say she would take the train to Santa Fe where her boyfriend would pick her up. She asks if I'm mad at her. I'm not but I kind of missed her yesterday. A paycheck for $415 for 9 days. That's $46/day. I'm not getting rich. But I get tips too. #35 says driver meeting I missed hinted that we might have to pay half of our gas. My thoughts turn to unions, impermanence, poverty.

23 days left until my big vacation.

News: Libya, Syria, flooding in Midwest, price of silver at record high.

April 26

Our winds may gust as high as 70 mph today. If hurricanes will be stronger then I guess New Mexico spring winds will be stronger too—more energy in the atmosphere.

TH says an economic crash is coming (2015?). Then: fascism or New Deal.

France gets 80% of its power from nukes. But 57% of the people say dependence on nuclear power should end. Fukushima on their minds. They have 58 reactors.

Peakwater.org. From FB link of Lora.

Back home, I get a call from Chris Rawlins, do some more guru yoga, listen to *Home of Happy Feet.*

April 27

Dream that "sweetness" is a category for rating apples in a mall survey. Sounds reasonable.

Samsara is a cold wind combined with being old & tired. I don't want to go to work.

22 days left until I can ration my energy toward dharma & creativity instead of this unfair ride business. I lose 4 fares today because our company doesn't accept credit cards. Ah, but I can practice as I work. Om mani padme hung hri...

Obama releases his birth certificate. He was born August 4, 1961, when I was a junior in high school.

A lot of sad fares today. Trish looked pretty through the thick glass but I didn't know what to say.

CP: Wild weather continues: giant tornado in Alabama; cresting rivers too. Sea surface temperature of Gulf of Mexico is 1 degree C. above average. Record highs in Galveston, Del Rio, San Angelo, Baton Rouge, Shreveport, Austin. Also record high minimum temperatures such as 79 in Brownsville. 4% more water vapor in atmosphere than 30 years ago. FL legislators kill renewable energy plan.

April 28

Younger Preston in dream. 36 degrees. See Gabrielle on walk; desire unspoken. The best girlfriend is the dharma. The best job? Dharma. I sing my old chant, "Thankyou for this, breath of life. Thankyou for this, moment of light. Thankyou for this, awareness of the universe."

Take Your Hair to the Maxx. So says her card. She's 48, likes to meditate. I call. She says yes to a movie sometime. She saw the Garchen Rinpoche movie in AZ.

#40 says nothing will change with ABQ Cab. One idea at the meeting was that drivers would buy all their gas & get 50% commission (now we get 29%). Hmm.

TH caller says there's a brown dwarf star in the solar system & it's causing global warming! There is a hawk with prey in a ponderosa by the bullpen. Wish I had my binoculars. I do Vajrasattva for all beings, especially those who will die with bad karma. The 100 syllable mantra.

Is anybody thinking long-term?

5 pm news: 280 dead in devastating tornadoes. First quarter growth was 1.8% due to harsh winter. Exxon-Mobil made $11 billion, up 69% from last year. Amigos Bravos versus Los Alamos Lab letting radioactivity into Rio Grande. Endangered dune sagebrush lizard hated in the Permian basin. Rep. Steve Pearce, oil man, says "the environmentalists' agenda is to destroy a way of life." Alabama: no mention of global warming. "God was watching out for us," says a woman. But not for others. I wonder how the crops are doing.

CP: web searches for info about hybrid vehicles have shot up 100% compared with a year earlier. Eyes too tired to read.

April 29

Sunrise at 6:42. I'm glad I can see it. And the Sandias. Out my east window. Beep says tea is ready. Time for *Heart Essence of the Vast Expanse*.

Shannon must live through climate change & degenerate times. And I may be reincarnated on earth too. We are all in this together. Suffering together, as zen friend in Ohio says. Solution: practice resting in the vast nature of awareness, rely on a lama, be kind.

I'm bringing *Mind Beyond Death* to work today. Dzogchen Ponlop Rinpoche.

A pretty fare: desire unspoken. She wants to go to the PowWow by herself. Makes me feel like a kid. Dusty wind again.

TH, Dr. Ravi Batra says oil will crash. Does he know about peak oil?

I call Maxx again but her "dance card" is full for the weekend. Garage sale at RigDzin Dharma tomorrow. Maybe I'll drop by but there's nothing I want but Maxx's love. Hahaha. The three "ha"s: Budd-ha, D-ha-rma, Sang-ha.

Ponlop Rinpoche says to die everyday. Fare asks "is God mad at us with all these storms?"

NPR reports that Obama toured Tuscaloosa. Wildfire forecast high for us. Iran is Syria's ally. I go into Whole Foods to pee. Marie hasn't had a chance to listen to my CD but it's on her stereo.

Saturday, April 30

NYTimes: death toll 333 in South.

To P.O., bank, garage sale at RigDzin. I talk to Lisette, give CD to Maxx. It's windy & cold. I buy some incense & a picture of Garchen Rinpoche. He will be here soon. The photo I have from years ago is nice, of him in a cave, but the new one is a close up of his face. Then I pick up Nick. I show him the Solar Disc sculpture on Zuni where he takes a few photos. We eat & get organized to send out demos of my songs. I make a list of songs I've yet to record:

"This"
"Sometimes I Wonder"
"Angels"
"Infinite Mothers"
"Baby, Call Me Baby"
"Circle of Love"
"Deeper than Skin"
"Anne, Can I Be Your Man?"
"Easter"
"Every Moment"
"I Live for You"
"I Thought"
"In a Dream"
"Let It All Go"
"No Blood for Oil"
"Om Namah Kali Ma"
"Sacred Voice"
"Secretly Hoping"
"Tears of Light"
"The Dancer"
"The Tao of Now"
"Yours"
"The Force"
"Easy Listening"
"Mirror"
"The Center of Your Heart"

2:15, I'm tired; I didn't sleep that well. Who publishes Bruce Cockburn? Don Henley?

3:15, I do dishes as Nick does fancy computer work. His father is 53, a ranger at Coronado National Monument. Nick wears black plastic glasses & has a shock of black hair above his brown face. Last name, Sedillos. He gets a call from David from Copper Mountain. We've got a demo ready to send to Sweden.

And here's David, smoking a cigar in his white SUV. His manuscript for book is called *The New Noetic Revolution* or something. Nick is editing it. David writes in long-hand & then Nick types it up. Complex philosophy. This is the 25th revision I think. They stand by the SUV as David explicates. I'm ready to take Nick home & go to Whole

Foods. Off goes the SUV with license plate VIDYA. Sanskrit for "awareness."

I will be vegan this week! Only buy vegan food.

Rent a couple DVDs at Hastings. Now I'm watching *127 Hours*. Aaron is stuck in a narrow crack in Canyonlands with his arm pinned by a rock. Samsara. Drinking his own piss, hallucinating. He cuts off his arm to live… True story.

The warming is global, the suffering mobile, the blind lead the blind to the edge of the cliff, the drama of karma it is what it is…idea for new song.

Then I can't fall asleep until 10:30, wake at 4. Back to sleep at 6 till 8:30. I guess I was too excited by the day & the movie.

May 1

Windy & cloudy. May Day.

"Nuclear power is neither clean, nor sustainable, nor an alternative to fossil fuels—in fact, it adds substantially to global warming. Solar, wind & geothermal energy, along with conservation, can meet our energy needs." —Helen Caldicott, MD, in *NYTimes* op-ed.

Call Sue. She had a nice week with Rick, birding & biking & going to vegan restaurant. Rick & Bob travel tomorrow, to the Smokies. We hope they don't clash.

Walk in a cold wind. Put heater on & watch some NBA, Grizzlies–Thunder.

ABC TV: Mississippi River & Ohio River meet at Cairo IL, record high water. Corn, beans & wheat threatened by plan to save Cairo by barge with explosives to breach levee.

Then, *The King's Speech*. Excellent bio-pic.

May 2

Dream of Asia, formerly known as Amy, gorgeous & petite. We're both at a group home near stupa I think. Play guitar, making up song, but people are too close, jostling my elbow…

Osama bin Laden killed! In fortified enclave in Pakistan city. Did they kill him without hatred? Buried at sea…

I'm off work today!

69

Mail out two demos at P.O. I now have 16 Go Green Stamps with tips on them: buy local produce—reuse bags, fix water leaks, share rides, turn off lights not in use (my dad was big on this one), choose to walk, reduce our environmental footprint USA—step by step, compost, let nature do the work, recycle more, ride a bike, plant trees, insulate the home, use public transportation, use efficient light bulbs, adjust the thermostat, maintain tire pressure & vote Democratic. (I made up the last one.) The USPS has reduced its facility energy intensity more than 28% since 2003.

ABC TV: "The Death of Public Enemy #1." Navy Seals rappelled from helicopters. Giuliani felt revenge he says. Cheney has lost weight.

FB: links to MLK & Khenpo Khartar Rinpoche on compassion. Did Pakistan build the compound for Osama? Taliban wants revenge.

May 3

Poodwaddle.com says the total number of humans ever born is 106,735, 546,967. I go for my walk and the number is up to 106,735,555,135.

Osama bin Laden is dead —but not global warming.

Fresh snow on the crest but it's to be 70 today & soon 84.

Working again. Mark: you go to church, Bird? He tells me of end-times. I say I'm a Buddhist. Mark: what do Buddhists do? Me: meditate. Mark: I meditate on Jesus. Nice guy, ex-prisoner saved by Jesus. No tip though.

I'm reading Ponlop Rinpoche & a print-out draft of *Diary of an Eco-buddhist*, my most recent title for this book. Two short fares in 2 hours but then it changes & I get busy. Mostly alcoholics.

Trish in the office befuddles me again. I ask her out again; too busy. Such kissable lips!

Chapter 5
The Children's March

May 4

Dream of standing on tall monument watching intramural football below. There is a perfect pass to me but I don't see till too late. I'm holding 3 photos of gurus, including Ngakpa Yeshe Dorje Rinpoche (the "Weatherman"). Another guy there who pisses from the top of the monument —on the photos! I do Vajrasattva purification mantra. He jumps all the way down; I carefully descend. There's a music festival going on but I want to see little Shannon.

NYTimes: "UN Forecasts 10.1 Billion People by Century's End." "The implicit, & possibly questionable, assumption behind these numbers is that food & water will be available for the billions yet unborn, & that potential catastrophes including climate change, wars or epidemics will not serve as a brake on population growth."

Definitely—not possibly—questionable.

"Survivor of Dust Bowl Now Battles a Fiercer Drought." "Boise City, Oklahoma, has gone 222 days with less than a quarter inch of rain in any single day…"

Mockingbird over by Marsha's.

Work. Fare is a Tea Party leaner; his wife too. They think Obama is evil (anger at stupidity boils inside me). They're Glenn Beck fans!

Three prajnas: understanding, experience, realization. Need to work on patience.

In love with teenager who waits with her group at the airport. Long brown hair.

Another Indian. I tell him it's the last time I buy alcohol for anybody. Then: bearded guy from the corner by McDonald's with his lunch. He says he is "God Almighty" & he wants to go to Hooters. Very sharp schizophrenic, he reads out the meter as we go. He notes that the meter is called "Silent 610." "God is pissed," he says. He pays up but I have to tell him to take his burger wrappings with him.

Chris calls back. His knee is hurting very much. He doesn't know why.

Dead Already But Not Dead Yet—title for book? No. *Deathwise?* No. Need to have balance of worldly & dharma.

Future: Pika will go extinct on Wheeler Peak, our highest mountain. Wheeler Peak climate will become that of Taos. Taos, that of Santa Fe. Santa Fe climate will become that of Albuquerque; Albuquerque, Phoenix. Phoenix? You don't want to go there…

How about *Fool's Paradise—Part 2? We Must Change Our Lives? Peak Worry.*

Fare says NY state rainfall for April was 3 times the record!

Trish moves me again. I stand by the window & say "wow!" I tell her of my music business. Should I tell her I wrote a song for her?

May 5

Dream of two Dawas (my deceased dog), Shanny.

Anne Klein audio on FB: "reality is vast."

16 days, 6 hours & 18 minutes to go. *Mind Beyond Death.* Slow day today after yesterday's big day. Cab-driving posture: laid back. I stand, walk around a bit, but…yawn.

Later: an Amish couple from PA. I take them from Amtrak to Super 8 on University. They're on their way to El Paso & Mexico for a doctor. They own a horse & buggy in PA; speak Pennsylvania Dutch.

Trish can't do anything this weekend.

CP: Bill Gates is pro-geoengineering & pro-nuke. Renewable energies such as wind or solar power are set to surge by 2050, & expected advances in technology will bring significant cost cuts, a draft UN report showed on Wednesday. Soil washing away.

AH

May 6

I dreamed that Mom was into dharma & going to do Sukhasiddhi or Sukhavahti practice. Was OR in there?

Humidity for May 4: 5% at 6 pm. Precipitation for year: .14 inch; normal is 2.10. 105 degrees in New Delhi. Will I see a billion humans die? Or will I die first?

Cab 448 is a solar oven but with nothing cooking but me. A greenhouse but with nothing growing but me. I wore shorts today.

Bullpen has precious little shade, as does the city. But since I'm the only one in here now I get some shade & roll the windows down. Not bad.

Kicking the Climate Bucket? No. *Diary of an Eco-Buddhist: Die or E of an Echo-Boodist.*

AP: "Crude Hits the Skids—Economic Concerns Send Oil Price Below $100 a Barrel." Is that good or bad news? Is this samsara? *ABQ Journal* editorial: small nukes sound good.

I call Maxx. She's in a meeting, calls me dear. As OR said, don't try too hard.

My song: the morning is global, the truth it is noble, the food it is local, focal, total, the cause & effect, the economy's wrecked... Needs work.

2, CNN Radio: flooding Mississippi, Memphis, al-Qaeda says Osama a martyr. Fare: government over-regulates—he liked Fred Thompson in last presidential election. ExxonMobil is over-regulated? The Koch Brothers? Caller to Randi: Oklahoma is a lost cause politically.

Mind Beyond Death is so wonderful. I'm on the dream bardo chapter now, illusory body. Yesterday is like a dream. And so is today! Look in the rear-view mirror of the cab: that Ford SUV is not really there! And I'm not either.

Santa Fe River is one-third normal flow.

Saturday, May 7

Matthew Fox on "New Dimensions": Catholic church is corrupt, fascist...

Ecobuddhism sent you a message. "Can America Feed China?" by Lester Brown. Great Famine of 1959–61 killed 30 million Chinese. China now imports four-fifths of its soybeans. Brown paints a portrait of an over-populated country out of touch with its water & food. It's an anthropocentric nation (aren't we all?) cut off from nature. My mala (prayer beads) is from Wu Tai Shan in China. APR was there. All beings are connected: Om mani padme hung. He concludes: "Like it or not, we are going to be sharing our grain harvest with the Chinese, no matter how much it raises our food prices."

One more vegan meal & I reach a week. 21 meals of veganism. The chickens & cattle are a little happier. Population control for farm animals! Plantpeacedaily.org.

Practice phowa as instructed by OR: "Bless me & others so that just as this life is over we will be reborn in the Land of Great Bliss!"

Nick is getting his mom chocolate for Mother's Day. I'm missing my mom (& also Maxx & Trish & Marie). We record "Yours" & "Nobody Knows."

86 outside. I lie down after dropping off Nick (& $30) & going food shopping. Read *Mind*, do AH.

66% of Pakistanis don't believe OBL is dead. Beale St. in Memphis is under water; 100 roads closed. Whales beached in FL. Polar bears in Manitoba usually have 2 cubs; now they are only having one. It's a Mother's Day story on ABC TV News. They report that ice is melting but not that their sponsor, oil, threatens the cute mother bear they show.

NBA, PBS. MLK & James Earl Ray. Who was I in 1967? A new hippie…

May 8, Mother's Day

Wake at 4, up at 4:30. At 8 I get up again from restless rest for the benefit of Mr. Kite & all beings. All I need is love; nothing's gonna change my world. Youtube. In 67 I was a Beatles fan & I still am.

I call Christine & wish her a happy Mother's Day. She's hiking up Atalaya Peak by herself. Chris is going to the zen center. Then I call Helen. She's also a mom. I go to Copper Mountain where Carol teaches the first session on our lineage. She recently went on a 10 day retreat at Tara Mandala & felt the power of the lineage she says. Carol is a good teacher. Old Geraldine asks if she could become a dog in next life.

Then it's a drive to Highland High School. Akilah is there by herself with signs & youthful energy & bullhorn. She's 16, with braces, goes to Albuquerque Academy prep school, is an climate activist, has a long braid & glasses. We see a roadrunner.

It's an iMatter march against global warming. There are signs like "iSuck/iMatter" (a coal plant), "iMelt/iMatter," "iBike/iMatter." I eat my peanut butter & jelly sandwich in the car as I write. Are all Buddhists eco-Buddhists? I think so, especially Mahayana Buddhists who wish to save all beings.

At 16, I never heard of ecology or Buddhism. Her little brother arrives, Kiernan, age 11. I ask him questions. He thinks his sister's activism is awesome. His dad is an engineer; mom, a biologist.

I sign the iPledge: to reduce my own CO2 emissions by as close to 5% as possible this year, in accordance with the latest scientific prescription for solving the climate crisis. There are over 100 marches happening in the US & in over 25 countries.

I find a dead warbler or something. It must have flown into the side of the high school. It's beautiful: yellow breast & rump, with a rufous crown, gray all over. I show kids the small bird. Talk to Heather, a high school student, who tells me of BEMP, Bosque Eco Monitoring Program. Leave the little bird by the wall & join the march. There are some adults too beside me, including Akilah's mom, Carol, & Lora Lucero. I have an iMelt/iMatter sign with the outline of an iceberg. Around 70 of us walk about 2 miles to UNM. Here are some of the chants we did: Our climate, our future, we matter, say what? (that was a good one) What do we want? Climate justice! When do we want it? Now! Why do we want it? We matter!

Not much traffic on Central. It's windy & warm. But kids vs. global warming is happening, thanks to Akilah. Another chant: We think the world must be told/ Climate change is getting old/ Our future matters, that's the truth/ So listen to the voice of youth!

We make it to the Duck Pond where mother duck & ducklings swim & there is food & drink. A display of data from climatecounts.org, e.g. ratings of fast food places for their climate awareness: Starbucks, 54 out of 100; Darden, 44; McDonald's, 36; Yum Brands, 30; Burger King, 11; Wendy's, Arby's, 7. I meet some more people, eat an apple, give my "One Earth, One Sky" DVD to Akilah. The videographer, Vanessa, is interviewing. My turn. She is a senior in high school. She asks me if I think there is hope. I say it's like a race between pollution & clean energy & right now pollution is winning. We need alternative media; I tell her of climateprogress.org.

Back home I look up the little bird. It's a male Virginia's warbler, length 4 & a quarter inches. *Vermivora virginiae*. I wish I could have heard him sing. Remember the kids: serious Olivia; the cute Dandelion Princess; the statuesque brown Latina. See you next time!

Chapter 6
Different World

May 9

Eggs again, from Lori's Farm. At least, they are local: P.O. Box 9891, Albuquerque NM 87119. Finishing them up soon.

NYTimes: Japan Reaffirms Nuclear Energy Use; Democrats' Plan Would Offset Deficit by Ending Big Oil's Tax Breaks.

Money can't buy me love; make it better.

The boss says OK to time off. I put it in writing for him. Back to work August 8 (but I could change).

The AC is nice but it melts the ice. No, I don't want to write another global warming song. Maybe it could be a warbler song: pretty little thing, wish I could hear you sing.

Price of gas down to $3.59 at one station. Wind is strong today. Dust in my eyes. That gust was 70 mph I'll bet. Albuquerque: The Windy City. Will it be a ghost town some day? Ghost city. Deserts are merging in China. *Mitakpa*, Tibetan for "impermanence." Rest now in empty awareness…

How long will this diary book be? A year? No, too long. And the subject is too urgent.

In love with woman in Lovelace at the information desk, where I have to wait for my fare. Nice Spanish accent & smile.

The mountain disappears in the dust; the tumbleweeds roll.

"With no satisfaction, even wealth is poverty." —OR

May 10

Dream of Australian "mammals."

NYTimes: In a Changing Antarctica, Some Penguins Thrive & Others Suffer—Relentless warming is taking a toll on Adelie & emperor penguins. "The mean winter temperature of the Western Antarctic Peninsula, one of the most rapidly warming areas of the planet, has risen 10.8 degrees F. in the past half century…"

On my walk I find that a cop has shot & killed someone on the next block. Om ami dewa hri.

At my job I think about the unintended consequences of supporting myself & transporting people. All the CO2. Wish I had a new Leaf & the grid was clean. Yes, no one really intending to destroy the biosphere. It's an epic tragedy; the hubris of technology. The road to hell is paved with good intentions.

Good news & bad news. Buddha nature & lower realms.

Alan Gomez, 22, was holding a couple at gunpoint when he was shot by a police officer. It was at the rental where my old haircutter & her little girls lived.

At home, two teenage boys knock on my door. They sweet talk me into a $38 subscription to *Vegetarian Times* magazine. Then Sue calls. She & David had a wonderful trip to Boone NC for niece Anna's graduation from college. Anna's boyfriend has a band, Do It to Julia, who will play at the Hardly Strictly Music Festival in San Francisco.

May 11

Wake at 2 but get back to dreams.

Do It to Julia on YouYube. What a bleak name. It's from Orwell's *1984* re rat torture. I'm not impressed.

Pretty little thing, I want to hear you sing, so fly over here & sing your song so clear…sing your song now dear…

Will flooding of refineries lead to gas going up again?

First fare, from University Mental Health, was locked up for saying she felt like dying. Formerly, she was a kundalini yoga teacher. Take her out by Black Mesa…

I want to hear it; I want to get near it…cold gray skies…

Mississippi River rising. CP says 6 states with record April rain: IL, IN, OH, PA, KY & WV. It's a biophysical interaction. O2, CO2. Fossil fuels are stored C from living plants. We burn, add O2. CO2 into the atmosphere where physics of warming takes place. But the news is limited to human-to-human interactions mostly. Expand your minds, humans!

A truck driver to Asian Massage. He has a pinched nerve. Asian woman comes out & touches me & says she loves me. She wants $30 for a massage. I'm trying to make money not spend it & I'm determined to keep trying on this slow day. Monks are working next door at the temple.

Slow everywhere in town; a little rain. Two months since Fukushima. It's still hot there.

May 12

Dream of hovering over pee-wee football game.

I play a bit; order *Masters of Meditation & Miracles*. If I didn't have to drive I would lie down. How will I finish book? I pray for strength. It's a beautiful day. Windy but nice blue & white sky. A beautiful dancer; a sweet old lady. *Tonglen* for them & all. A man going to Surya Das retreat in July.

Vajra body: *tsa, lung, tigle*.

News: levees holding in New Orleans. Alan Gomez was only holding a plastic spoon when he was shot by cop.

AH.

May 13

Thankyou, hen. Thankyou, hen. Thankyou, hen. Three eggs for French toast. No more eggs for a while.

Humans for 10,000 generations. Genus homo for 100,000 generations. We have been "modern," i.e. non-hunter-gatherers, for only 600 generations. Two generations ago my grandfather saw the transition from horses to automobiles.

April CO_2: 393.18 ppm. March global temperature up .88 degrees F. from March average in 20th century. Just that much so far, & so many impacts.

Albuquerque Police Department has shot 14 people in 12 months...

Beyondnuclear.org. Paul Gunter says Fukushima unit 4 is leaning badly with 100 tons of nuclear waste on top. Unit 1 has had a core meltdown. The concrete is reacting & releasing CO_2 & H_2, with an explosion possible. Hot groundwater, seawater...

My cab airbag warning: Death or serious injury can occur.

TH: financially we have to hit bottom before there can be an awakening. No gain without pain. Steve Earle has a new CD, *I'll Never Get Out of This World Alive*. Ninth Friday in a row of Syria's brave people protesting.

Home to FB from Maxim: meat-eating destroying the earth. China aiming for 50 gigawatts solar by 2020 instead of nuclear. The 6 reactors at Fukushima made 4.7 gigawatts.

Saturday, May 14

Journal: "Want a Prius? Get Ready to Wait."—"Some buyers will have to wait until April next year for deliveries of the latest Toyota Prius because of shortages of a new battery that's adding to production delays from the March earthquake & tsunami in Japan" (Lithium-ion battery).

"Spillway Opening OK'ed"—25,000 people & 11,000 structures threatened but better than another Katrina for New Orleans. Crops flooded. Cotton price up 86% from last year; corn, 80%; soy, 39%.

To the library where I finally get my turn to check out *Eaarth* by Bill McKibben plus a Steve Martin comedy. Home to water the fruiting mulberry etc. *Mimus polyglottos* reminds me of Florida. Now what would bring the most benefit to the most beings? Read? Write? Play music? Meditate? I will lie on the floor & listen to the mockingbird with the front door open. Such busy energy. Seemingly happy. But he doesn't know or care about me. Only humans can know all beings & care about them. Then I read preface to the new book: "total rainfall across our continent is up 7%…"

To friend Craig's daughter Erica's Anthropology Department graduation. I like Jennifer, Craig's sister. A big wind gust breaks up our picnic but we were ready to go anyway.

News: River still rising; Obama wants to drill more. Samsara. 63,000 acres is the size of the fire in the Gila National Forest. Cheerful Royale Da reporting.

Eaarth: "We may, with commitment & luck, yet be able to maintain a planet that will sustain some kind of civilization, but it won't be the same planet, & hence it can't be the same civilization. The earth that we knew—the only earth that we ever knew—is gone."

Thank goodness for Steve Martin.

May 15

Long dream of Amma's presence, being held by people. Someone goes to get NYC Ballet book. Alphabet: Malalayam or Tibetan? Amma sweetness.

It may be that the best way of helping beings is to meditate. Compassion needs joy. I go to Copper Mountain where 7 of us do the Green Tara practice with food offerings. Om tare tam soha. Then, a walk in the bosque. Intense azure sky & intense cottonwood green leaves. Riverrun, mountainfloat.

CP: "Is Obama's call for more drilling bad messaging masquerading as cynical policy —or vice versa? Return of the environmental-problem-that-must-not-be-named." "Scientists alarmed by diseased fish in Gulf." "The Vatican says to take climate science seriously."

Talk to Sue & mention that if she wants to visit she should come when Amma is here in June.

May 16

Concepts of tiredness, age.

NYTimes: "Record Water for a Mississippi River City — Vicksburg." Krugman: GOP radicals in the House are holding US hostage over raising the debt ceiling —will Obama stand firm?

Nine days left in the unsustainable transportation business. At least, when there's no business we're not warming the planet. Donnie, #48, has no motivation to come to work other than paying off his boat. His wife isn't the outdoor type.

Come down from your tree, I just want to see, remind me of beauty evolving through time, remind me of beautiful thoughts in my mind…

An environmental clean-up instructor from Alabama tells tales of tornadoes & power outages. She gets her electricity from a TVA nuclear plant. I say it's good the tornado didn't take out the power to the nuke, as in Japan. She remains pro-nuke however.

TH on the fundamentalist threat in the US. News: excessive three poisons. *Journal*: "Energy Efficiency Rules Targeted" by the Martinez administration, rolling back Gov. Richardson's green legacy. I'm reading *Eaarth* in between rare fares. Not much I didn't already know but it's well-written. Good on peak oil & how coal use will increase. "Making a Life on a Tough New Planet." Blurb says the book may restore my faith in the future. Hmm.

Fare works for Canadian Forces & is here for training in mass disaster forensics.

In an unusual little prayer, I ask OR for a title for this book. *Even Though the 3 Realms Were to Be Destroyed, There Is No Fear—Diary of an Eco-Buddhist* occurs to me. Nice, but it's too long at 13 words. Om mani padme hung hri.

CP: April hottest in Central England in 350 years of records. Alberta floods. Colombia: 11 months of nearly non-stop rain displacing over 3 million people.

May 17

Dreams of kids & dharma & music.

So, the "Rapture" is to be Saturday? How many believe this crap? *Doonesbury* is making fun of it. There's an electronic billboard about it too. I thought it was an ad for a heavy metal band.

I go to my counsellor, Jon. Good to talk. Remember Pilar when I see her: older, cute, probably Catholic.

Buddha Touched the Earth—Diary of a You-know-what.

Eight days to go. *Eaarth* is depressing. So many will have such a hard time, including Shannon & Aaron. Try to summon bodhicitta, including joy. Maybe Shannon & Aaron can discover inner joy. I write song, sing. Now I'm behind a hybrid Coke truck: good news or bad?

Home to *Eaarth*. I'm too tired to do much on email, CP or FB. But there's a message from APR: "Relax!" Rest after dinner, then some guru yoga.

May 18

Wake with dry mouth. Dream of camping with Preston. Up at 5 after hearing all-night DJ's sign-off song "Always Look on the Bright Side of Life" by Monty Python. "Life's a piece of shit, when you look at it..." Full moon in the west; robins in early light. *Ngondro* plus Medicine Buddha. OR, thankyou!

Mahler's 5th Symphony. Then birdjam.com mockingbird. "Males sing in Spring, & both sexes sing in Fall, although female song is usually quieter." Haha, what a jammer!

Fare: "It's a different world than I grew up in." You can say that again.

McKibben recalls "there was a White House gathering for a man advocating 'Buddhist economics'..." Jimmy Carter hosting E.F. Schumacher. Bill pans "doomers." The other possibility is "we might choose to manage our descent." "We're moving quickly from a world where we push nature around to a world where nature pushes back—& with far more power. But we've still got to live on that world, so we better start figuring out how."

Judgement Day? T-shirt wearing people downtown. Should I go back & see? No, save the gas.

Amma followers in cab. Then I get a break. Stand by the cab writing. People motoring through the drive-thru for their Teriyaki Chicken Bowls (just as I used to do). It will be a cold day in July before I eat chicken again. Smell of grilling chicken flesh, mass-produced death & waste.

Get Real—Diary of an EB. 7 days, 3 hours left. Craig calls back: Jennifer is too busy to date she says. Then, a reeking fare, an old black man. Smells like shit but he gives me a $13 tip. NPR: complex obscurations. Lisette, Lisette, do you want to bet...

Home to call Rick. He hiked 32 miles in the Smokies & saw a huge tulip tree. Borderline hypothermia. Big Creek. He says Bob brought a gunny-sack full of placebos, his vitamins. But they had no major clashes.

May 19

Some rain, cold. Dzogchen Ponlop Rinpoche on YouTube: Rebel Buddha, his new book. APR message: "relaxed openness." But I'm tired & afraid. Last fare was a drug-related young girl with baby & cigarettes. Shanny, if you're reading this, may you be in a state of relaxed openness. All emotional obscurations come & go...

How do I take "dharma" as my girlfriend? Relaxed openness. Open to women...

May 20

Nice update from Shannon on FB. They're subletting Sean's house by a hot spring. No time to see her before they go to wedding in CA though. She's busy, working.

Precipitation yesterday was .05 inch. That makes us .19 for year, with 2.40 normal. Mostly zero in the state yesterday. Fire restrictions in forests. Active hurricane season forecast. Catalpas blooming. Yuccas too. BAU for the 20-something guys flying to San Diego for a bachelor party. Then they go to LA & back here. All powered by the "last days of ancient sunlight" (thanks to TH).

I finish chapter 5 of *Mind Beyond Death*, "Evaporating Reality: The Painful Bardo of Dying." "A pure realm is not necessarily an actual world or planet; it is a state of mind where we can achieve enlightenment. It can be on this earth or in a different universe. It does not matter. We aspire to that. That is always the best thing for us, & it is also the best thing for all other sentient beings."

Encouraging words from a grad student in English: self-publishing is actually the way to go.

Not BAU for guy on oxygen having trouble breathing. I take him to VA ER.

Four & a half days till I can unbend my knees & uncoil my spine.

Negative? Positive? Real.

Comic book movie filming in Chilili. The news is too bleak; people want to escape with comedy shows on TV, cop shows, ads. Gizmos. Play *Angry Birds*. Music. Get real. Rapture? Any second could be your last, but you must realize true nature of mind is emptiness. Otherwise, it's not really your last...

Trish says I can call her but she's so busy...

Saturday, May 21

I'm tired after walk, waiting on tulsi tea.

The Rapture/Doomsday author, Camping, is 89. I'm sure thoughts of death occur to him as to me. "Faithful Student Song" reminds me of death every day.

Nick comes over. Two demos ready to go then FB page for Copper Mountain. My knees hurt; my ego hurts. But I'm getting some things done for a change.

CP: "While cutting education, KY gives $43 million tax break to creationism theme park."

Helen is sick so there will be no phowa practice tomorrow. OR is having health problems so we should do 21 Vajrasattva mantras a day. I read some hagiographies from *Masters*.

May 22

It's amazing to have a thought; amazing not to have a thought.

NYTimes: Record high snowpacks in Rockies & CA, OR, WA. Not in NM or AZ. Floods threaten; Lake Mead & Lake Powell will rise. FB: Lora Lucero attended a 4-hour civil disobedience training. "I believe the failure of our US government to address climate change in any meaningful way will require peaceful civil disobedience in order to force our leaders (aka followers) into action." I comment: some people are doing it—when the conditions are ripe it will happen I hope —vote out the deniers!

I call Preston. He's fed up with Obama's secrecy & treatment of Bradley Manning. His work at the veterans' national call center 800 number is frustrating. Veterans want loans but the VA doesn't have the money. Preston may not visit after all this summer.

To Copper Mountain. Complex words on lineage. Carol cries. Devotion. Then we do chod. The four line ter from APR. I offer my body etc. to my guilt demons & 5-poison demons... Carol, David, Gretchen & I go to Saigon Restaurant. I kind of like Gretchen but she lives in Taos.

CP: TX lawmakers are set to slash funding for the agency responsible for fighting wildfires in the midst of a historic wildfire season in which some 2.5 million acres have burned. National Academy of Sciences says the median annual area burned by wildfires is projected to jump 100% to 500% over much of the West by mid-century. Republicans control all 3 branches of government in TX. Real adaptation is as politically tough as real mitigation, but much more expensive & not as effective in reducing future misery.

Craig & Sue call back. Craig has forgotten his Amma mantra; I recommend he get another one. Sue says maybe I could rent Rick & Bob's condo for $400 a month. I could save on rent. I'm so tired. She's thinking of coming to see Amma!

May 23

NYTimes: "City planners in Chicago are choosing different types of trees & pavement materials after climate scientists have advised them to prepare for a wetter, steamier future." Another story: "Global plastic production is expected to continue to rise inexorably from the estimated 250 million tons churned out annually now." Hmm. What about peak oil? How many people will be left in US in 2100? One million? 500 thousand? Doomsday is gradual. Most of the time.

Monster tornado hits Joplin MO: 89 dead so far, 30% of town destroyed.

So, I've got to strike it rich, find cheaper housing or move to FL or find roommate. Or keep driving. Or sell the 800 CDs I still have. Or find a woman to take me in.

McKibben: "we'd be wise to turn vegetarian..."

Death is good; it can increase one's awareness. Even if you don't buy reincarnation, death focuses the mind. Even death of a planet.

CP: Japan is considering a plan that would make it compulsory for all new buildings & houses to come fitted with solar panels by 2030. World loses one third of total global food production to waste.

May 24

Dream of girl's corpse, rotting. Other girls wake her.

Email from Sue: she's coming June 15. Amma will be here June 17!

At age 20, Garchen Rinpoche joined the Kham Resistance Fighters to take up arms against the Communist Chinese invaders of Tibet. He will be here June 2. Also a newsletter from Dzogchen Nyingthig. So wonderful. Magical, powerful, compassionate APR. A new guru yoga practice included to do in addition to the one in the *ngondro*.

TH: WTO says US can't sell "dolphin safe" tuna anymore. And now Walmart's countdown to Memorial Day...

Eaarth: "In a world more prone to drought & flood, we need the resilience that comes with 3 dozen different crops in one field, not a vast ocean of corn or soybeans." Localize.

APR is building a Copper Mountain temple in Tibet to prevent war & other calamities.

Here's an idea: Big Bang makes magic possible. Since all beings were one at the singularity that exploded into our universe, all beings are still one in a way. All connected. All evolved. Some are totally tuned in to this, such as APR, OR & Amma, my big three. So, get real. There is lots of suffering but it's all like a dream...

It's to be 88 degrees Saturday. I wonder if cab 448's AC can cope with that. I wonder when the guys come to turn on my swamp-cooler at the house. OK, KS & TX on tornado watch. I give 2 CDs to Cecelia & Jeff. "Wind turbines & rooftop solar panels could provide 81% of NY's power..." writes Bill McKibben.

"I may look like a farmer, but I'm a lover / You can't judge a book by lookin' at the cover." —Bo Diddley

May 25

Dream of coming up on a ladder through the floor of an office where I'm given tincture of "drew" as medicine. I knew it would happen. Erik Drew translated the new guru yoga text. Drop of dew equals "drew." Also dreamed I was playing music.

NY 26 goes Democratic. Stephanie Miller on Ustream showing her blue eyes.

To work. A truck of Rasband Dairy, 873-2171. Maybe I should call them up & ask about their carbon & methane footprint & what happens to the bulls. TH says that if Republicans self-destruct, Obama will have a super majority & could be like FDR. Wouldn't that be nice? But the collective karma is peaking...

Chris calls. I'll go up to Santa Fe on the train & spend Saturday night.

Henry, #32, quit, after fight with Bill the Dispatcher.

Here it is, my finished song called "Virginia's Warbler": Pretty little thing, I want to hear you sing, so fly over here & sing your song for me, fly over here & sing your melody, I just want to hear it, I want to be near it, I just want to hear it, I want to be near it. Come down from your tree, I just want to see, remind me of beauty evolving through time, remind me of beautiful thoughts in my mind, remind me of what I forgot as a kid, & all of the good things that I ever did. *Vermivora virginiae. Vermivora virginiae.* Just watch where you fly, you don't want to die, the fish in the ocean are swimming around, but that's not for me see I don't want to drown, I'd rather be singing way up in a tree, like you I could sing & be flying so free...

"Get real" says McKibben, speaking of the dullness of the new life on eaarth & offering the internet as excitement & aid in mitigation. I'm into the net but I don't think life will be dull for a long time. I finish the book. What about spiritual help for the sick & dying? Are friendship

& family enough? What do I have to offer? Well, Medicine Buddha practice, phowa, the wisdom teachings that it's all a dream-like illusion. "Eaarth represents the deepest of human failures. But we still must live on the world we created—lightly, carefully, gracefully." A poignant closing sentence. Is Bill, a Methodist, implying some kind of grace from God?

What can Obama offer the tornado victims? Is Christianity enough?

May 26

White, red & blue light; I bow to APR.

NYTimes: Storms Create a Scramble to Install Shelters. New Mileage Stickers Include Greenhouse Gas Data. Hope Rises as Waters Do Not.

There seem to be more mockingbirds this year. I used 130 kilowatt-hours of electrons in April & 17.36 therms of CH4.

I'm waiting for Dori. "This could be the last time, this could be the last time, this could be the last time, I don't know." (Rolling Stones.) She advises me to totally relax on my vacation. I advise her to go see Amma. Hug her goodbye at Walmart. Trish is working 70 hours a week now. 232 missing in Joplin; 125 dead.

A petite woman with a "Native Cutie" T-shirt. From airport to Hard Rock Casino & Hotel (owned by Isleta Pueblo). She's from Alaska, lives in DC, a lobbyist for Indians, busy on her phone. Then, Luz. Sexy as hell, from Colombia. Display of skin, display of mind.

81 degrees in Fairbanks says *USA Today*. Miller Fire in Gila is 86,000 acres now. Yemen turmoil.

Home to PBS excerpt from film on North Korean escapees: famine & fascism. But then excellent news from CP: GE sees solar cheaper than fossil fuels in 5 years.

May 27

Dream of nice woman. Rainbow Gathering. Hunger.

Here comes the sun. How about only good news today? It's alright. Ani Jetsun Ma Rinpoche singing with Tulku Gyurme Tsering. The possibility of enlightenment within this moment grows with every mantra, every prayer, every gap between thoughts.

I turn the water heater down to between "warm" & "vacation" since I'm still hot from my walk & summer is coming in.

To my last day of work. I am a low profit driver. I am a non-prophet writer: future depends on our actions. Karma. I give Thanh-tam a CD. She is a beautiful (married) midwife who delivered two babies last night on the graveyard shift. She is delighted. I tell her meditation is always hard at first but you have to stick with it. After she goes to Tucson, I sing almost my whole CD to myself. It amazes me that I wrote it. Then a physics professor, here to speak on dark matter. It's everywhere he says, along with dark energy. Invisible beings too I wonder...

Church sign: "Pray for Rain." But pray without grasping I say. Out to Rio Rancho to get the dance instructor. She works for the owner's gay son at Enchantment Ballroom. She never tips but I get a $10 tip from my last fare. Time to go see Gloria at the gas station. I tell her she has to stop smoking. She say she knows but she can't. High five bye-bye.

Nothing but good news. Delicious ayurvedic dinner to celebrate.

Home to hot house. Cate says she had to reschedule the swamp-cooler men. Sit outside with the happy crickets.

Chapter 7
Fire & Love

Saturday, May 28

Light & birds. Dreamed I was playing second bassoon—Bob was first! I was very tentative, not having practiced in a long time.

Left knee hurting now. How did I get to be an old man?

CP: Memorial Day, 2030—"The three worst direct impacts to humans from our unsustainable use of energy will, I think, be Dust Bowlification & Sea Level Rise & ocean poisoning: Hell & High Water. But another impact far more difficult to project quantitatively because there is no paleo climate analog may well affect far more people both directly & indirectly: war, conflict, competition for arable and/or habitable land... Sadly, the chance that humanity will avert catastrophic climate impacts has dropped sharply this year. (See 'the failed presidency of Barack Obama, part 2.') And that means it is increasingly likely we face a world beyond 450 ppm atmospheric concentration of CO2, which in turn means we likely cross carbon cycle tipping points that threaten to take us quickly to 800 to 1000 ppm."

My goal is to double mantras now that I'm not cabbing, from 10,000 to 20,000 per week. In between writing & life.

Now I'm on the Rail Runner approaching Santa Fe & the Southern Rockies. "It's not too bad riding backwards" says a kid a couple of rows ahead of me. How many mpg per person are we getting? A touch of snow on Santa Fe Baldy.

Chris should be waiting at downtown station. I wonder how he's walking with his swollen foot. I've got the *OnEarth* magazine for him with the book review on how annuals threaten food supply. *Empires of Food* by Fraser & Rimas, reviewed by Rich Manning, author of *Against the Grain*. Manning is pro-perennials in poly-culture.

We go to national cemetery & I show him the tomb of Dennis O'Leary, died April 1, 1901. He committed suicide after going AWOL to carve his tombstone, a self-portrait.

We go to the cinema, *Cave of Forgotten Dreams* by Werner Herzog. It's about the oldest cave paintings, recently discovered in France. They are 32,000 years old. Cave-bears & rhinoceroses & beautiful horses & a bison-woman.

Christine is in the Grand Canyon with her daughter & others. Chris couldn't go because of his knee & a foot with gout. He picks lettuce from his garden & we eat pizza under the stars & think of the good old days in Flagstaff.

May 29

Dreamed I had a girlfriend to kiss. She cleaned up cat poop. Yesterday recycled. Oh, there's a present for me, from Mom. It's a belated Xmas present. Whatever you celebrate: happy & happier. I hug a little girl in a choir robe.

We go to Mountain Cloud Zen Center with lettuce in Chris' cooler. Two hours of sitting & walking. There are 4 of us. Then hurry to the train on time. Time flies. I like how the train is a shared experience, a little community. Off to the west, the white stupa stands out among the buildings.

Home to the computer. "An Unlikely Power Duo Emerges in the Global Fight Against Climate Change." Bill Clinton & Michael Bloomberg are organizing the cities of the world. Tim DeChristopher to be in Santa Fe on June 13. I google "miles per gallon per person." Here are some stats. Cyclist, 600 person miles per gallon (calorie equivalent). Bus, 160 pmpg (40 passengers @ 4 mpg). A 75% full 747 jet, 30 pmpg; cruise ship, 10 pmpg. Walking, 360 pmpg in calorie equivalent (80 kCal/mile). A Chevy Volt in full electric mode may be more fuel-efficient than walking for more than 4 passengers! Colorado Rail gets 448 pmpg.

NPR. Obama visits Joplin. This year there are more "wedge" tornadoes. Albuquerque news: gusts of 50 mph possible. Memorial Day stuff honoring the soldiers. What about "blessed are the peacemakers"?

Sue calls. They went to Eustis to see niece Kelly & the kids. Sue plans a car-free day tomorrow. "Too Darn Hot" by Ella Fitzgerald. 89 degrees in the bedroom at sundown. I open all the windows & put on the ceiling fan. Who needs a swamp-cooler?

May 30

Memorial Day. Lady Gaga on YouTube. I can't understand the words but I think it's Christian, pro-LGBT. Freedom to disco, "Born This Way." Mockingbird near house. Their range is surely extending northward. I write brother Jon a birthday card with a polar bear on it. Great music from my computer library. AP News: airline fuel costs going

90

up with $100 a barrel oil. 22 gallons per 1000 miles per person comes out to $330 per passenger in fuel costs on a round-trip NY to LA.

"Our experience is unique to our makeup because everything is mind, & mind has no absolute existence; therefore it has no fixed way of appearing." —*Mind Beyond Death.*

Tim DeChristopher (Bidder 70) is facing 10 years in prison on 2 felony charges for derailing an illegal sale of public land from the outgoing Bush administration to private oil & gas developers. Sentencing will be June 23. Tim's church, Unitarian in Salt Lake City, supports him. A sign at a rally reads "We Are All Bidder 70."

Two hour nap after lunch. Then to Whole Foods where granola has gone up 35% in a week. Home to do more guru mantras.

FB from Lora. Guardian: "Emissions from energy fell slightly between 2008 & 2009, from 29.3 Gt to 29 Gt, due to the financial crisis." But last year, 30.6 gigatons of CO_2 poured into the atmosphere. The recession didn't give us much breathing room. BBC: Germany to end nuclear power by 2022. PBS: flooding in ID, MT, ND & SD on Missouri River. 520 killed this year by tornadoes. Jeff Masters from Weather Underground says the trends in heat & heavy rain are global warming. Pope still against condoms for AIDS prevention but his church does help AIDS victims a lot.

May 31

Dream of a music fest at Ngakpa Yeshe Dorje's stupa or some place like it but there are stupas all around. He was known as the Weatherman because he could control the weather. He said he once made it snow in Yellowstone to put out a fire after I told him about it. Dream of kids, friends, fire.

NYTimes: Groundwater Depletion is Detected from Space— "from 2003 to 2010, aquifers under California's Central Valley were drawn down by 25 million acre-feet—almost enough to fill Lake Mead, the nation's largest reservoir." Great Tim DeChristopher speech to Power Shift 2011. Akilah was there. "Now is Our Time to Take a Stand."

It's a car-free day for me. OR is feeling headaches & pain in body. Do Vajrasattva for him says Helen. Get to work on *Get Real* book. My eyes are tired but the goal of a finished book is bright before me.

After dinner it's the Heat versus the Mavericks. My eyes burn. The Heat overcomes.

June 1

Dreamed of OR, in yellow shirt, swimming, seen from roof of a hotel. In Florida? Also, a woman doctor prescribing new meds for me & a marching band of kids.

Shanny, dear daughter, says she's back in Taos after California wedding of Ben & Em. Hung hung hung! Blurry clouds & hazy mountains. Water & walk.

Part of me wants to just do guru yoga rather than dealing with climate triage. Triage is the process for sorting victims into groups based on their need for or likely benefit from immediate treatment, when limited resources must be allocated. Peter Gleick writes: "In coming years, we are going to be faced with increasingly difficult decisions in that must now be called 'climate triage'—choices about who & what is going to be protected & saved, versus abandoned & lost."

TH has RFK Jr. on. West Virginia mountaintop removal mining. 2500 arrests recently occurred but there is a media blackout. See thelastmountainmovie.com. It's the first day of hurricane season. El Paso breaks its own record with 118 days with no rain.

To Whole Foods at 3. Pang of love: Marie waves to me. It's my karmic wind agitating me. It's that wonderful skin & twinkle in her eyes. It's all natural. I mutter I love you, Marie, even though I know it's hopeless. Go home to write, meditate.

June 2

Dream I'm driving a bus. It's a part-time, temporary job. I take a break & climb with others down a rickety construction of branches, down a gorge. At bottom, sex workers & a guy named "Microbe." Camping. But I've got to get back to my bus or I'll lose my job.

Light of spontaneous lama.

NYTimes, Lester Brown: "When the Nile Runs Dry." Family planning & education for girls. More water-efficient irrigation technologies. Plant less water-intensive crops. Ban land grabs by foreign governments & agribusiness firms. "Rising bread prices could undermine Egypt's revolution of hope & competition for the Nile's water could turn deadly."

I go to the Construction Industries Dept. hearing. It's packed. Lora is there. Joan Brown too. Shrayas from the Sierra Club. One commissioner in a suit listens to testimony. Gov. Martinez wants to roll back the energy efficiency standards so thoughtfully put in place under Gov. Richardson. I take notes as the speakers almost unanimously oppose Martinez. Sally McCarthy of the Sierra Club says the smoke in the air is from an Arizona fire. Exacerbated by climate change. A climate scientist from Sandia Labs speaks of long-term catastrophes. Mary Westerland mentions *Collapse* by Jared Diamond. Is anybody really listening? Are we just preaching to the choir? I get a little mad & start clapping loudly after each testimony. Then realize it's wasted energy. In love with a woman sitting on the floor who is serious but emits a great smile every now & then. Find out that her name is Susan.

I go to Cate's after lunch with my late rent check. Her granddaughter is there, plus a kitten & Maurice the cockatiel. Cate cries thinking of going off into the desert to die because nobody cares about her. Her house, where I live, is underwater, worth $80k now, less than her mortgage. She can't sell.

Later, an Environment NM guy, Joseph, knocks on my door. They are trying to get Otero Mesa to be a National Monument. He says there are no jobs in Los Lunas where he's from. I sign up for $15 & give him some water. I call brother Jon on his birthday. He's 62 on 6-2.

Garchen Rinpoche. At South Broadway Cultural Center. He briefly introduces the movie of his life: hello mother-like people, we are like family. Ina, from Austria, translates. Karma, Tara helped him through prison. Then the movie. He's in continuous pain. Eyes, body. But always happy. He spat in an official's face in prison.

We come out of theater to smoke, smoke all over the city. The plume of smoke is from Alpine AZ fire. So says the scroll under the NBA finals. Dallas wins in an amazing comeback.

June 3

Complicated dreams: I take a cab; Bill is the driver. Only $1.14 on the meter even though he keeps driving in circles. I give him a $5 tip & then he comes into the store where I work.

Ngondro: craving Susan, the woman from meeting, tired. Outside there is ash from the fire on my windshield. Wallow fire is 106,000 acres now.

93

NYTimes: "Experts advising the UN said renewable sources could deliver nearly 80% of world's total energy demand by the middle of the century." Is that fast enough?

Do more guru yoga. Guys to work on swamp-cooler show up early. Now I'm ready for the heat.

Eat as a billion people starve.

"Oxfam Predicts Climate Change will Help Double Food Prices by 2030: 'We Are Turning Abundance into Scarcity.'"

"How to Find Happiness in Today's World": Garchen Rinpoche talk. I'm not very happy as it starts. In church on Louisiana there is a good crowd. I hope OR gets a crowd this big some day. GR says worldly system for happiness & religious system for happiness are like two eyes wide open. Work & meditate. Mind the same for all beings in the six realms. Develop love, extend to all mother sentient beings not just those you like. Be in love with love; be adverse to adversion. Melt the iceblock of self-grasping with the warmth of love for all beings. Wonderful words but I'm still depressed, self-grasping. Into just going home to sleep.

June 4

Wake at 3:51. *Longchen Nyingthig ngondro*. Sunrise in smoky haze. Fire at 120,600 acres now. Computer is depressing. *Newsweek* piece from Lora on how we are past tipping point on climate. I cling to Susan from meeting. Amma, come soon & take me in your arms.

To Garchen Rinpoche. He gives the empowerment of Milarepa. Excellent energy. Lunch at Orchid Thai with Helen, Michael & women. Helen says OR might have found a church to buy for his dharma center. Afternoon with GR: let go of thoughts...

Go home in 90 degree temperature to turn on swamp-cooler. Check from Sue who is managing my money for me. $5k. I put it on my shrine & do some guru yoga, inspired by GR. After dinner, I read the chapter from *The 100,000 Songs of Milarepa* about Bardarbom. It contains the origin of my old song: my mind is big as the sky, bright as the sun, strong as the mountain, deep as the ocean! Garchen Rinpoche explained it so well.

June 5

Dreamed I played bassoon again. Played a lot, including "Teddy Bears' Picnic."

94

Ann Klein responds to my request for the other translation of "Prayer for Extreme Times." She must be done with her retreat. Translation is pretty much the same. Dawnmountain.org: "The awareness of the fleeting nature of life brings forth compassion."

"More & more affluent homes in the suburbs are buying electrical generators to use when the power fails." —Nicholas Kristof

9:30, off to see the lama, the wonderful lama of love. There I meet Tilia, enthusiastic newbie with a great smile. I sit by her. She takes refuge. The afternoon requires a long 3 hour sit as we hear more about love & compassion & mindfulness. Then we line up with white scarves & offering envelopes to get our individual blessings. Before we part, I get Tilia's number. She is probaby 4 foot 10 inches tall, Hispanic?, blond-brown hairdo, ring on pinkie, 50?

HEAT. 102 in Houston. 25 cities break records. News, then more NBA. Dirk Nowitski makes his 37th straight free throw.

June 6

Wake at 3:30. KUNM music then up at 5:30 after NPR's bright side of life spin on weather disasters. I want to tell you, dear reader, that I tried to do something to prevent your disasters, to mitigate the pain, to help you try to adapt, to help you through the ultimate disaster of death by telling you mind goes on...

9:30, call Tilia & leave message. Dharma-lover?

I had a nightmare about food prices going up on farm. Then I'm loaded with gear & guitar in a city. Shannon & her friend go off. I try to reach her by cell, take a swig from a wine bottle.

Am I having a post-guru let-down? I go to office for a paycheck, then take 2 checks to the bank.

CP: James Hansen says "The US Department of State seems likely to approve a huge pipeline, known as Keystone XL, to carry Canadian tar sands oil (about 830,000 barrels a day) to Texas refineries unless sufficient objections are raised." Estimated 200 ppm CO_2 in them...

Bodhicitta could save the planet! And you, too!

Unborn no-mind.

Will T. call? Rick calls. He has the heat on; Sierra ski resorts to stay open until July 4. He says there is too much environmental info to keep up with. I agree. The reality is changing faster than the science can keep up with.

I walk to the corner after dinner in heavy smoke, the smell of pine burning 200 miles away. Inciweb says Wallow Fire now 233,522 acres. There are 30 large fires burning in the US today; 4, very large: 2 in AZ, 1 in GA/FL, 1 in AK.

No call from T.

June 7

Dreamed I had forgotten to fill in logsheet for cab except for the prices so had to try & remember pick-up places & destinations.

Wake at 3:30 again, up at 5. Only do 500 mantras, feel faint. Back to sleep after early breakfast then wake at 9:30. Listen to more crazy Stephanie Miller, walk. Visualization. "Letting go of this life is the Bodhisattva's practice."

A car-free day, just like billions of people every day. Shower-free too. 0% containment on Wallow Fire; 2500 people fighting it.

NPR: Obama concerned about economy; intensive strikes on Tripoli. Local: hazardous air quality advisory through Thursday morning. I'm going out for a walk anyway. Wallow: from carbon sink to carbon emitter. Smoky all the way to Iowa. PBS: talking heads down on "Obama's" economy; 30 year anniversary of AIDS, 30 million dead. Red sun high in the sky. Then NBA. Tired but I watch to the end of game in which Nowitski is playing with a 102 degree fever. Mavs win.

June 8

Dream I answer test without studying. Also, with a full backpack, I head out of a place where there are 2 weird guys into Native American stuff. They are very messy householders. Head out of city to Florida camping.

Wallow, 311k acres. Wildlife?

Thomas Friedman quotes Paul Gilding: "When you are surrounded by something so big that requires you to change everything about the way you think & see the world, then denial is the natural response. But the longer we wait, the bigger the response required."

I recycle, then water in the desert (hollyhocks are a lovely pink). The sky is blue for a change. I think about going to mountain forest

96

ecosystem but that would use 2 gallons of gas (12 pounds). I would make 40 pounds of CO_2 which dries the sky-island forests through drought. It's very warm at 10. It would be nice to go to the shady trees around Cole Spring at 7500 feet. But it would be better with Tilia or Lilia or Wilia. Twice the pmpg.

Write R., call Helen.

Noaa.gov: two thirds of NM is in extreme to exceptional drought conditions. Three months ago, none of NM was in extreme drought.

NPR: OPEC balks at increasing oil production except for Saudis. Pressure on Weiner to resign for his "digital sexcapades." Fire at 600 square miles, that's a ten mile strip from here to Santa Fe. It threatens power lines; rolling blackouts possible. Erratic winds up to 50 mph; smoke cloud up to 30k feet. Local: 13 fatal shootings by ABQ cops since Jan. 2010. PBS: Bruce Babbitt speaks out about Obama's silence & GOP attacks on environment. ABC: two thirds of US at 90 degrees or above. Get used to it says climate scientist, Heidi Cullen. TX has 5500 square miles of fires. Heat waves kill more people than tornadoes & blizzards.

New title: *Buddha Nature* or *True Nature—Diary of an EB.*

I turn off swamp-cooler. It's bringing smoke into the house.

Helen calls. Phowa retreat in September in Crestone. Steve at Albuquerque Manor for his Parkinson's. She's going to Denver tomorrow. Shannon texts that she'll call tomorrow.

June 9

How about *Emergency Buddha?* 36 football fields a minute of tropical forests lost (NRDC). How many football fields a minute of ponderosa & animals are the monster firestorms destroying?

Emergency Enlightenment, that's better. Beyond hope & fear.

"Nowhere Man" in E. "You're Killing Me" in Gm.

Maxx gives me a good haircut. She drove GR & monks & housed them. Went to AZ & back. She's going to DC for Kalachakra empowerment by the Dalai Lama. Carbon footprint.

I cancel meeting with Nick. Feeling tired eyes, smoky throat. 2 hour nap.

Shannon calls. Aaron got a car from his grandmother. She loves me & I love her. I look forward to seeing her next week. And my sister. And Amma!

Tilia calls! She's floating she says. From GR? But she's busy, no movie this weekend.

June 10

Sleep till 6.

CO_2 for May 2011 at 394.35 ppm. Annual 2010 at 389.78 ppm.

SongwritersBestSong.com charges $10 per song. Nick says it's not worth it.

I walk, buy paper. I become sad: "State Pulling Out of Wolf Program —Commission Vote a Win for Ranchers." Martinez appointees. Wolves only predate 2.4% of cattle; coyotes kill 26%. (Humans account for 100% of wolf killings). I say people should not eat meat; birth-control for cattle; restore the wild. 69% of New Mexicans support wolf reintroduction. Are there wolves in NM when you read this? Anywhere? Imagine the future...

1.2 million wild camels in Australia. Methane producers, 100 pounds per year. Equivalent to a ton of CO_2 each. One sixth the amount of an average car. I say kill the cars not the camels! Birth control for the camels...

"Heat Takes Toll, Kills at Least 7." Om ami dewa hri.

Just took ibuprofen after lying down. Am I dying? Yes, slowly.

USA Today: 4m acres burned this year in the US, more than double the average. Cool La Niña to blame somehow. 26.7% of contiguous US in some form of drought (9% last year). Lake Okeechobee at record low. Michio Kaku: Fukushima meltdowns almost turned into 3 Chernobyls.

Elk on the run from Wallow fire. Fascism in Syria; refugees in Turkey. Record snowpack in Western US, 200–700% normal.

Call Sue. She didn't sleep well last night due to worrying about cat with chin infection. She did yoga today & looked up birding sites in NM! I do phowa, long life mantra.

Saturday, June 11

Wake at 3 with dream that someone was calling a comforter by the name of "Velorian" when it clearly said "Versace" on it. I get up & do "Vine of Faith," lie down & listen to radio. Get up again for *ngondro*.

AP: "NM panels roll back environmental initiatives"—"A state commission voted Friday to repeal NM's energy efficient building codes, becoming the second panel of gubernatorial appointees to move in as many days to roll back environmental initiatives that had been pushed by former Gov. Bill Richardson."

Amy Goodman in op-ed quotes Naomi Klein on climate change refugees: "This crisis will be exploited to militarize our societies, to create fortress continents."

Nap for an hour or so until Craig calls. He's going to Denver for a baseball game. Idle, polluting rich. Hazy & hot. I go to Whole Foods. Marie is there but gone when I'm done with my calzone. Maybe I'm becoming more realistic about women now...

Tim DeChristopher interview in the *Alibi* plus a letter from Lora. He found himself in a position to put in a phony bid on oil & gas leases to keep the fossil fuels from being drilled. He faces ten years & $750,000 fine for fraud. Are we a mass of lemmings going over a cliff? Amber & Shrayas going to see Tim plus Lora, Akilah & I. One car?

Lonely walk. Extreme times prayer.

June 12

Dream of useless hippies, bad economy. A magic rock with writing on it.

I'm lonely until I get to the guru yoga section of *ngondro*.

Thomas Lovejoy in *NY Times*: restore ecosystems, reforestation, mix CO2 with seawater to make cement...

Cate calls! She wants to go to Copper Mountain. Patience is the Bodhisattva's practice. I was going to walk in the bosque but I can change to walking later somewhere, maybe by library. The doves are cooing to each other. More humans, more fires.

Green Tara, all become.

Amma bhajans. *Crown of Skulls—Diary of an Eco-Buddhist*. Only a Vajrayana practitioner would understand that title.

Local news at 5: Wallow fire at 444k acres, 6% contained. Luna NM OK for now. Pecos water supply stressed by broken well. NBC: flash mobs getting violent in Chicago. Fukushima is 3 months old, Cesium 134 & 137 contamination.

NBA: Marc Anthony sings the national anthem. He is a great tenor! I call Chris; he's not walking. He's going to Paris with Christine at the end of July. "That'll kill a few polar bears," he says. He says I shame him with that. Me: you just feel guilty.

CP: twice down on *NY Times* reporting on climate. Reported infertility & impaired fertility are up among both men & women, regardless of age. US Chamber of Commerce supports chemical companies. Solar is ready now.

Fire has closed I-25 in Raton Pass says the banner under the game. Dirk & Co. win it all in 6 games.

June 13

"Unchanging, non-dual wisdom"—may all beings recognize it.

2 hours with Nick. Then mail from APR on his $17 million temple, Zangdo Palri, Glorious Copper Mountain. Amazing stories & prayers & aspirations. For all beings. Also in the mail: photos from Rick for Sue & I to share.

Now I'm at Foods. Marie says my CD is awesome. I'm waiting for Lora & Akilah. We're going to Santa Fe to see Tim DeChristopher. Lora drives.

Akilah sued Gov. Martinez with kids against global warming. She wants a future.

Newenergyeconomy.org is hosting Tim in Greer Garson Theater. They want to have Santa Fe eject PNM & have public power

He is 29. He says the most intense period of change that the world has ever known is coming. The paradigm of materialism has to be let go; growth strategy hasn't worked for most people. The economy must totally change so that it is just. In the future we will need each other. But the status quo won't give up easily. We must end corporate personhood. The Tea Party is based on dissatisfaction. What's next? Fascism or cooperation? The government is monitoring Tim's activities but he's not intimidated, not at all, even though Obama administration is pushing for a four & a half year sentence to make him an example to other would-be non-violent civil disobeyers. He is preparing for prison.

Akilah asks a question. Tim says it's time to make a stand for sustained resistance. The exit strategy should be that we win, not that we go home. I wonder how many are ready to make a sacrifice such as his. I still hope it's possible to vote the climate science deniers out of office.

June 14

Wallow fire now 452k acres. But sky is clear &·blue & the mockingbird is happy—somewhat. I clean up for Sue's visit, recycle glass behind Walmart. Dust to dust.

"APR, in 1992, was visited by a Dakini who revealed to him that this place is the Pure Land of Guru Rinpoche, known in Tibetan as Zangdo Palri. For several months after that, Rinpoche himself could see the Copper Colored Mountain Pure Land here. Yeshe Tsogyal also appeared to him directly & told him that the door to the Pure Land is here…

"May whoever offers money or their own abilities in the construction of the Mandala, or who takes only a single moment to delight about it, as well as any animals who happen to circle it, take on all the good qualities of its construction & go to a Pure Land.

"Over & above everything else, the most important thing in this work, & in everything we do, is our own heartfelt wish to benefit others, without exception. This is the Bodhicitta that is the basis of all our activities. This is why we are here."

APR saw *An Inconvenient Truth*. I send $108.

ABC: melanoma was up 45% between 1992 & 2004. FDA issues new rules for sunscreen lotions. BBC: Chilean volcano disrupts air travel in Australia. Twitter & FB are big in Indonesia.

Sue calls. She's packed, has to get up early.

Entertainment Tonight: Miley Cyrus is worth $15 million; *Spider-Man* Broadway, $70 million.

FB: Medicine Buddha was the first ritual practice in Tibet, & likewise it has been the first large gathering practice for OKL, OR's sangha…Atisha himself tells us that among the most beneficial practices we can do in the degenerate time (i.e. now) is the Medicine Buddha.

June 15

SAGA DAWA DUCHEN, Tibetan full moon festival of the birth, death & enlightenment of Shakyamuni Buddha. Positive or negative actions are multiplied 10 million times. Plus it's a lunar eclipse, so multiply by a 1000 more.

"All this world is but a play, be thou the joyful player" — Incredible String Band.

Sue's carbon footprint is increasing quickly as she flies. But she's coming to see Amma so there is great benefit too, especially today. I'm off to mail demos & pick her up at the airport.

Susie!

We go to the Rio Grande Nature Center, on her birdwatching list. It's peaceful. Wind in the cottonwood leaves, black-chinned hummingbirds at the feeders & hovering over the ditch. We find later that they eat insects as well as nectar. It's 95 degrees so we try to stay in the shade. A turkey vulture, woodpecker, Canada geese, green winged teal. I think I hear a grosbeak but the birds are hiding from the heat. Cottonwood fluff blows but there are neither clouds or smoke.

Extreme Times—Diary of an Eco-Buddhist. That should be the title.

With Sue & Cate to Copper Mountain. 12 of us do "Samantabhadra's Prayer" etc. then go to Namaste Restaurant for delicious food. Jane talks of reading the book called *Hot* about climate change. I get animated about practice being the only hope as we face death. What does Brian think of that, with a 2 week old baby girl? It's too loud in there.

Full moon over the city lights as we drive down the hill back into ABQ. I'm too arrogant & impatient.

June 16

Wake at 4. Up at 6. Daily practice.

Sue has cleaned the kitchen sink area! We have soy yogurt. I ask her if I was too preachy last night. She says no. We walk to the 7-11 for her coffee & paper. I read her excerpts from *Ulysses* (it's Bloomsday!) for an hour. Crazy, amazing novel.

We play the "Rebirth" game of throwing die & moving from the lower realms to enlightenment.

After eating salad at Whole Foods (where I point out Marie), we go to the Pueblo Cultural Center just in time for dances. The Red Turtle Dancers from Pojoaque do the Buffalo, Butterfly & Rain dances in the hot plaza area. Museum art viewing then home for a nap.

Low in Tampa was 82. Sue says I have to be rich or famous to attract a young beauty like Marie. Is it all samsara?

After dinner, we walk around the hot block, then call Rick, nature boy. Sue brings out the frozen yogurt. We watch old home videos. Cindy Moku, why didn't I fall in love with you? Suzuki Roshi says Buddha's attachment to beautiful things isn't attachment, it's Buddha activity. Sweet.

June 17

Mother's Day! That is AMMA Day! LOVE Day!

Sue & I get an Amma hug. Sue cries after it. She got a TM mantra once but Amma only gives mantras during Devi Bhava. Sue offered flowers; I, a tree to be planted. Amma was kind of busy & didn't smile at us, but her body was warm & blissful if only for a few moments…Om ah hung vajra guru padme siddhi hung…

Shannon calls: she's not coming down. She has to work tomorrow. So we'll go to Taos.

Shannon & Aaron meet us at the plaza & eat hotdogs. Gift shop browsing, then dinner at Orlando's Restaurant. Yum. Delight of fatherhood, brotherhood. To Sean's house where they are subletting. Then we walk to the nearby warm spring. Bats & stars come out. I pray to my teachers. Shanny & I sing my Amma song, "Om namah kali ma." Sue afraid of the bats. Silence as we dip our feet in the warm water.

June 18

Wake at sunrise on the floor of Sean's house. Pink sky. Others sleep. I practice silently.

Walk to the gate & back in happy solitude. Cool air; sun over the mountain at last.

When everybody is up, I play a little: "The Lamb," "Tyger, Tyger." Then it's off to the Purple Sage Cafe where my daughter works. Aaron eats with us. Shannon is our waitress & says our meal is taken care of. Sue tips her $20. Aaron goes to work at his restaurant; Sue & I go to Taos Pueblo.

Jesse, a UNM student in environmental engineering, gives us a tour. Beautiful mountains, cool air. Old town. US government was hard on them. We ask what the yellow bird is by the river but Jesse only knows the Tewa for it.

Sue sees her first magpies in Taos (*Pica pica*). We drive back by the Purple Sage where Sue orders a smoothie for lunch. Sweet good-byes... Always so quickly parted from Shanny.

We take the high road south, up into the windy forest. At a scenic view we try in vain to get a glimpse of the songbirds flitting through the conifers. I tell Sue that when she retires next year she could just hike off into the vastness... Snow patches on the peaks. I put on CD of Beethoven piano sonatas.

Down into the badlands near Cordova. A towhee in the pinon-juniper. But then: smoke near Santa Fe Baldy, a fire just getting started, white smoke in the dry wind. I've lived in the area for 29 years & never saw a fire up there. How do you like your oil company money now, Governor? The fire explodes & a huge cloud rises above us as we visit Shidoni Foundry. We see a pouring of molten bronze (temperature, 2100 degrees). Bird watching by the dry Rio Tesuque. We call Bob. He's not feeling well, perhaps a recurrence of his GRD.

We get to Chris & Christine's at 5:30 & decide on pizza & salad, the latter from their wonderful garden. We look at the fire's smoke cloud from the street. Chris is going to New Orleans to help his son find a place to live near Tulane where Orrie will go to law school. Mindfulness of speech discussed.

Home to cicadas; wind to be 50 tomorrow.

June 19

Take Sue to the airport. I will miss my dear sister. May we serve humanity, seeing the Mother in all beings.

Pacheco Fire is moving toward Pecos Wilderness & the Santa Fe Ski Basin. Cynthia Jurs has her bags packed in Chupadero, 6 miles up-wind. She says it's "a great meditation on non-attachment."

Nyigma (Kali Yuga) is the Age of the Five Degenerations: 1. lifespan, 2. negative emotions (the 5 poisons increase), 3. beings (it is difficult to help them), 4. times (wars & famines proliferate), 5. views (false beliefs spread). From Patrul Rinpoche's *The Words of My Perfect Teacher*.

Peak dysprosium will happen in 2011 according to *National Geographic*. But "ocean power farms might be just over the horizon." Do you say "echo" or "eeko" Buddhist? I guess I'll change my pronunciation to "eeko" since no one knows what an echo-Buddhist is...

104

Kumi Naidoo, global head of Greenpeace, before being arrested on an Arctic oil rig: "This is one of the defining environmental battles of our age. It's a fight for sanity against the madness of those who see the disappearance of Arctic sea-ice as an opportunity to profit. If we don't stop them, the oil companies will send in the rigs & drill for more of the fossil fuels that got us into this mess in the first place—in a place where the cost of a spill is unimaginable. We have to draw a line somewhere & I say we draw that line here today."

Smoky. Phowa.

June 20

Nightmare that false beliefs were taking over. Extreme times. Trying to protect a baby.

Shannon posted "Happy Father's Day! You are the best father I have ever had…"

Journal: "Sandia Trails Closed" (through Oct. 31 or until good rains come). "Fierce winds coupled with dry conditions kicked the Pacheco Fire near Santa Fe into high gear Sunday as it jumped from 900 to 3000 acres & raised a 30,000 foot-tall smoke cloud." "Unseasonably strong" winds. Big Tesuque threatened—where I was thinking of camping July 4th. My old stomping grounds…

What I'm presently writing in diary will become past when put into the computer. Even further past when you are reading it. Time's arrow, mitakpa. Only you know how big the Pacheco Fire will get. My actions today influence your actions in the future. What good is it for you, reader, to hear of past calamities? Maybe you weren't aware of them & you can generate compassion for the victims—as I am trying to generate compassion for beings suffering in the future. All beings are present. The squirrel that died yesterday in the Pacheco Fire is present in your moment, in one of the 6 realms. And the 4 immeasurables are always present in your mind. Mind's true nature. And Guru Rinpoche is present in APR, OR & Amma, because, as OR said, all wisdom beings are one.

I drive to Rio Rancho. Amma on CD. Devotion & sadness. Dr. Dalton is as efficient as ever, says my brain naturally likes to lie down because of my low blood pressure. In love with busty girl in the waiting room, office girl, little girl playing on the floor. Where's Pilar? Desire dissolves. Then I see Jon. He says he'll come see Amma tonight. He

105

thinks the word "extreme" is over-used, e.g. *Extreme Makeover* TV show. I ask Pilar out. She's with someone she says. I tell her she's very attractive.

Next: Costco for my three drugs. Walmart wins in Supreme Court, against class-action women employees. A million acres on fire in US. McCain blames illegal immigrants.

6:09, I'm in the token line for Ammachi, in love with everyone here. Virginio, my old landlord & an Amma devotee, is greeting people. 6:29, seated with token O-2. Video showing: *Embracing the World*, now about tsunami recovery. There's Nancy David across the room; Julia Jean passes. Amma gave $44 million for suicide prevention for India's farmers. Amma says science & religion need each other.

Amma comes in, blesses water as lively video of bhajans plays. Jai! Holy water is passed out. I put mine in a new bottle, a perfume bottle I buy for $5. Amma bows to everyone. She says we are the embodiment of pure love & supreme consciousness. External security can disappear in the blink of an eye, but internal security one can't lose. She says don't worry about the future, laugh. She tells funny stories with morals. Om parashaktiye namaha!

2:10, I'm leaving the hotel. Such happiness! Such energy! Such love! Met again Jim Dixon, Aaron's kendo teacher & father of beautiful China. Felt Amma's body embracing me & saw her look at me & smile, giving me a flower petal & a Hershey kiss. Got a massage, carrot cake & CD (*Love Is the Answer, Volume 1*) again. Gave the first one to Shanny. Bed at 2:30.

June 21

Wake at 7:30. Guru Amma on mind.

Wallow Fire is 51% contained at 519,319 acres; Pacheco Fire at 3800 acres, uncontained. 600k acres burned in NM so far in 2011.

Listen to Amma's song, "Everyone in the World" & cry. "Everyone in the world should sleep without fear, at least for one night, sleep without fear..." I learn the chords & sing it myself.

A car-free day & a 2 hour nap after lunch.

I finish off the frozen yogurt Sue bought. Mindless spooning while watching the news. Rick calls. I tell him of Sue's visit, Amma, Shannon & Aaron. He pulls weeds at Mount Davidson tomorrow in white-crowned sparrow habitat. Bed at sundown.

June 22

Dreams of lush blooming lilacs.

Climatesolutions.org: cool schools bill in Oregon. Mulberry sapling by the mailbox survives without water. But can I survive without physical love?

Inciweb: Growth potential of Pacheco Fire is extreme. Threats: Santa Fe watershed, ski area, Nambe Pueblo lands, Tesuque Pueblo lands & Tesuque Peak communications site. My beloved mountains. I post on Facebook: there is no compassion without wisdom; no wisdom without compassion... FB from Lora: McKibben planning civil disobedience to protest the Tar Sands pipeline, August in DC.

Call Sue. She had a hard Monday at work. Saw a raccoon tonight. There are puddles in Palmetto. Bob still sick. She is reading Amma's biography. I read *Mind Beyond Death*, call Tilia & leave message. Print maps for Denver. Sunset walk, no clouds. Neighbor Andy is miserable. Truck problems, broke. Blanca out walking Pecas & Cameron. Gabrielle's sunflowers bloom, towering above me.

June 23

I'm in the upper deck/upper bunk & catch a soft baseball hit my way. Dream.

Al Gore in *Rolling Stone*: "It (the climate crisis) is about whether or not we are still capable—given the ill health of our democracy & the current dominance of wealth over reason—of perceiving important & complex realities clearly enough to promote & protect the sustainable well-being of the many. What hangs in the balance is the future of civilization as we know it."

Souris River threatens Minot ND. Obama speaks to the nation on winding down wars. *Journal* says high to be 99, 7 above normal. We average 2.5 triple-digit days per year. Thought about going out today but don't really have to; wish T. would call back. I post "Amma on CNN" on FB. Pacheco Fire at 5500 acres, 10% contained, 10% humidity. Brahms & Stravinsky violin concertos.

Tomorrow I see OR again. Three gurus this month; that's what I need. OR for 4 days upcoming; GR for 4 days; Amma for 2 days. That's 30% of the month! And sister for 4 days!

They are rallying for Tim DeChristopher at Santa Fe Federal Courthouse today even though sentencing has been put off.

I'm reading *National Geographic* about how organized religion may have been the spark that started the Neolithic farming revolution. The archeological site Gobekli Tepe "suggests that the human impulse to gather for sacred rituals arose as humans shifted from seeing themselves as part of the natural world to seeking mastery over it." Charles C. Mann. "I think what we are learning is that civilization is a product of the human mind." Klaus Schmidt, archeologist.

An email from Dr. Glen Barry, Ecological Internet. Biocentric ecology news archive needs money.

I walk in the oven-like twilight. Mastery over the human mind is what we need...

Chapter 8
OR, Part 2

June 24

Budget Talks Impasse. Obama & other nations open Strategic Oil Reserves. Matthieu Ricard op-ed in *NY Times* mentions Himalayan glaciers at risk.

Michael comes for me at 9 am. He used to deploy nuclear missiles. He does the Sun Dance with the Lakota. We are driving to Denver. His wife, Helen, already flew there. We pick up Louise at La Cienega. She says bye to David.

White smoke of the Paceco Fire is lying flat toward Lake Peak. The Sangres look like the Smokies. Any bears in there?

We talk about dharma, diet. Out into pronghorn territory on I-25 North past Las Vegas NM. Patches of snow on distant peaks. Krishna Das on the CD player: Sri Ram Jai Ram. Brown grass. What do the pronghorns eat? Up through burned area at Raton Pass into Colorado. Eat lunches we brought at a Shell station. Michael tells us how one thing led to another & he got involved in the Cold War. He considers himself a warrior, defender of the tribe. But he is so instrumental in getting things done for dharma. I, on the other hand, am a peacenik, Vietnam having convinced me that our tribe (the US) is too aggressive. He went from Boy Scouts to the Army & is now in cyber-security; I dropped out of Boy Scouts.

North toward the megalopolis the population density increases. Into rush hour traffic, then Thai food for dinner with Helen.

OR in Zen Center of Denver, an old Christian Scientist church. Now it's transformed from black & white into the colorful world of Tibetan art; a beautiful shrine is set up in front. The empowerment of Medicine Buddha. Medicine Buddha had practiced one-pointed aspiration to attain enlightenment for all beings. OR's teacher, Tsara Dharmakirti, healed himself & others through this practice. Rinpoche wants to keep the lineage going. Many kalpas ago, Medicine Buddha said that during the degenerate time his name would benefit sentient beings. Medicine Buddha drubchens were the first practices done when Buddhism came to Tibet. We need bodhicitta & pure perception. See the world as the Pure Land of Lapis Lazuli. A symbolic empowerment type tonight. We end with Rinpoche asking the names of those he hasn't yet met. And a joke from a boy in the crowd: what gets wetter the more it dries?

June 25

A towel. I sleep at Josh's renovated carriage house. But people next door are outside talking all night. Dream that OR is called "sharman." I guess that's dreamspeak for "charming shaman."

Josh wants to ride his bike to the Zen Center so he loans me his car. I make it on the freeway, past the Broncos' stadium & to the Speer St. exit with no problems. The sangha assembles for the monlam, the wish path, or prayer gathering. Rinpoche teaches, then we get into reciting the text in English, followed by long mantras. I sit in a chair under a Medicine Buddha tankha. We are not eating meat or eggs & refraining from alcohol & sex for 3 days. My meds are in a basket on table near the shrine being blessed by the energy in the room. There is a list of loved ones to be remembered who are ill. I am still learning the mantra & have to check the text from time to time but slowly I become more & more focused. There are about 40 of us.

At lunch, Michael drives a few of us to the church that Rinpoche wants to buy. The black Baptist church members are having food & singing after a prayer by the pastor outside but we can go in the main sanctuary & look around. It's nice, with a dome rather than a steeple. The stained glass windows of Jesus will have to go. Ruben is with us, a young investor who says he will donate a lot to buying the church.

Afternoon session includes some very still moments. Seven-year-old Trevann practices with us. Around 6 we're done. Rinpoche does a little dance on his way out before Melissa grabs him. Then he pokes me in my big stomach as he passes.

8, just drove to Josh's. He & Clara are watching a movie on a laptop; the kids are in bed. I realize I have left my meds in the basket at the Zen Center. I do have valerian though, to help me sleep. It will be OK to miss my meds for one night. As Rinpoche would say: perfect!

June 26

Slept better (no neighbors) but with vomiting shit nightmares from the valerian. Maybe that's part of the healing. Up at 5:12 to do *ngondro*. Meet Bodhi, one of the twins. So cute. Rinpoche spent the night at the Zen Center, sleeping on the floor, & did extra sessions with a few hardy students. Someone asks him if he slept. Probably, he answers. He did mantras in his sleep.

He wants us to do 7 long mantras a day as a daily practice. How many are we doing during the monlam? I'm sure not counting. It's so nice to just forget about doing anything else & concentrate on the syllables & the prayers for all beings.

During afternoon break, Alaya is dancing around, Rinpoche is cutting out paper things to fill statues with later, Ananda is lighting candles, John is watering the wonderful flowers. Melissa arrives running; Ruben is on his BlackBerry. It's hot outside but in basement of the solid church it's cool with fans on. I talk to Angela a little, former nun, good-looking nursing student. She hasn't heard of APR's planned Copper Mountain Temple.

Helen drives Michael to the airport; he has to get back to work.

Dinner with 4 guys at the Thai Basil again. Dharma tales. Chris C. thinks he remembers my friend Chris from the Jemez Zen Center. Back to help stuff statues. Guru Rinpoche in my hands, I clean him outside & inside. Then Chris & I wind a red & yellow thread together. But I'm tired & drive home soon.

June 27

Slept well, on meds. Dreamed I was driving my old truck & it had steering problems. Also, trailer park violence; find Mom in a trailer. The big stupa in Santa Fe had been moved for repairs; lots of plastic retreat huts there but I can't find Norma, only cats.

Body, speech & mind karma has accumulated for kalpas. Posture & prostrations are for body karma purification. We purify speech by recitation; mind, by silent mantra.

Ananda reads some last names of the sick & dead. Rinpoche tired from being up till 12:30. Lunch with Lenny who does loving kindness meditation all the time he says. He has his first interview with Rinpoche. Alaya is bouncing on mattresses; Ruben gives me some goji berries. Tina introduces herself: nice blond hair, smile.

Afternoon session. And then we're done. Impermanence. Remember bodhicitta says Rinpoche.

Dinner at his house, with Louise, Johanna & Patrick, Nina, Helen & Rinpoche's big brown dog. Rinpoche says extreme times are worsening but that Vajrayana is spreading. He doesn't seem too worried by the

111

extreme times. I ask about bodhicitta & guru yoga connection. He gives me a simple answer. I ask him if he ever had Christians try to convert him. He says he told a Christian that Buddhists believed in God but not a permanent God. (did he mean gods?) Rinpoche says he smoked 80 cigarettes in one day when he was 11 & got very sick. Also, he got drunk when he was 7. Louise, in touch with David in Santa Fe, says there's a fire near Los Alamos. Everyone but Johanna & I are eating steak. Louise doesn't want to leave but I'm ready to sleep.

I drive Louise to Myra's in the dark & see a fox after I drop her off. Trotting along the sidewalk in a residential area.

June 28

Eggs & toast with Ahni, Bodhi, Maitri, Josh & Clara. Ahni is 5; the twins, 2. They like the PBS show *Dinosaur Train*. The kids are wild for a while, then Ahni shows me her plastic mala that Rinpoche gave her & recites her mantra (Manjushri, for learning). She is so sweet. She asks her mom if we can play her cello. Then the kids are off to summer school camp & I'm off with Louise & Helen, rolling down the interstate, the two women in front, talking. 90 pmpg.

Helen suggests that Louise read from her notes, so we have a discussion, then listen to Helen's new CD of Rinpoche doing the long Medicine Buddha mantra. Amazing how focused you have to be to get it right. But the coffee-drinkers talk over it.

Look at mountain. Is there a glacier there? Not anymore. Impermanence implies emptiness. Implies forms can arise. Implies Vajrayogini visualization for guru yoga. Implies enlightenment…flashes of it anyway…And Medicine Buddha form, sound & compassionate mind is emptiness too, I realize.

Louise buys the paper in Vegas: Los Alamos Under Seige, Blaze Threatening City & Lab, Could Triple in Size in Coming Days. Also, Vegas worried about water. As I drive us toward Santa Fe we can see some smoke visible in rain over toward the Birthplace of the Atomic Bomb. We arrive at the La Cienega exit just as David does. Welcome back to samsara he says. Bye, Louise!

Home to hot & dusty house. FB: Angela likes Bird Thompson (the music page). That sets my heart aflutter! I water the thirsty trees. Sue calls. She & husband had a nice trip to Micanopy.

112

June 29

Start 7 long Medicine Buddha mantras per day. Write on FB: Bird Thompson likes Angela. Get paper. Jay Coghlan of Nuclear Watch NM doesn't think the fire will burn the 10,000 drums of radioactive waste at the lab. It's now 60k acres & growing fast. Concepts of hope, concepts of fear. Wildlife? No, it says wildfire. Why do they never say anything about the wildlife? Our fellow beings…Concepts of samsara, concepts of nirvana…

Inciweb: Pacheco Fire at 10k, 20% contained; Wallow, 538k, 93%. The Los Alamos fire is called Las Conchas. It's 3% contained. Overview: fires in US all along the dry south, from west to east.

Mail copies of APR brochures to Angela. She replies on FB: keep on liking me, yourself, everybody. A good Buddhist answer.

Local news is all about the Las Conchas fire. There are 7 fires in the state.

June 30

Dream: a long Threepenny Opera.

"May I see samsara with all its endless activity as a prison or a pit of fire!" Then there's the "wisdom of no escape." Or maybe the only "escape" is to see the prison/fire as a Pure Land…

I vow during *ngondro* to have only tea for dinner. Practice for upcoming *nyungne*. And lose some gut.

Good op-ed in NY Times: "Fire Up the Grill, Not the Atmosphere"—"Food is responsible for 10 to 30% of global GHG emissions. By many estimates, cooking represents more of a meal's carbon footprint than transport. For certain vegetables, it accounts for more emissions than agriculture, transport & disposal combined." Brian Palmer says that microwave is 40% more efficient than pan-frying on an electric stove.

Before you get too sick or too old, learn to be still, practice the 4 immeasurables & the 6 perfections.

I call Nick. His message says "I love you." He calls back & we set a time for recording. That means I'd better practice guitar & singing. We'll plan video too.

113

I remember only 43 people from the monlam. Is that all there were? I find OR on youtube, discussing emptiness at Naropa. Share it on FB. Wow! Here he is!

A Conservation Top 11 from the Wildlife Conservation Society: 1. Chinese alligator 2. Tiger 3. Wolverine 4. American bison 5. Humpback whale 6. Andean bear 7. Andean condor 8. Elkhorn coral 9. Gorilla 10. African elephant 11. Kihansi spray toad (WCS.org) They are assisting all of these animals. But global warming threatens us all.

Las Conchas fire spares town & lab, no danger of radiation. *Journal*: "Dona Ana County farmers are making an urgent plea to Gov. Susana Martinez for water for their thirsty crops. If they don't get the water, the Elephant Butte Irrigation District is slated to close down for the season July 5, after slightly more than a month of irrigation. The season typically starts much earlier & ends in September or October."

Brahms' amazing violin concerto.

Democracy Now. US drones operating in 6 countries—labor strikes in Greece & UK—drought in Somalia area is producing climate refugees; 10 million people at risk of famine. Christian Parenti speaks on his new book, *Tropic of Chaos: Climate Change and the New Geography of Violence.* The military takes global warming seriously. Counter-insurgency doctrine seeds world with crime & social breakdown. World needs positive adaptation. Poppy uses one-fifth as much water as wheat. So farmers in Afghanistan adapt to drought. Stop the tar sands; stop coal.

Las Conchas fire at 93k.

Sit with eyes open, eyeballs still. Do 1000 mantras of unborn awareness. Emaho! I bow to OR!!

R. writes: awesome retreat at Tara Mandala. She signs it "love, R."

How green is your internet? YouTube shows 2 billion videos per day, which equals 4,000 tons of carbon dioxide. Internet equals airlines in terms of GHGs. Google energy is investing hundreds of millions in wind, solar & high-flying kites. Unfriend coal is on FB.

No dinner. Go out front, barefoot in sand, for sweet breeze at sunset.

July 1

Dream of scrape on my nose. A bit dizzy—maybe I shouldn't do *nyungne*... Worries of health, meds that make me dizzy. How will I do at 10,000 feet with only one meal a day for a week?

Outside: smell of smoke, hazy breeze from the north. Ten fires in NM now, including 72k Ruidoso fire. Las Conchas fire at 100k, largest in NM history. It's on Santa Clara Pueblo sacred lands now. Higher Power, grant me the serenity to accept the things I cannot change; the courage to change the things I can; & the wisdom to know the difference. Buddha, Dharma & Sangha: may I have the wisdom to see things as they are; the compassion to love all beings; & the union of wisdom & compassion.

July 2

Dreamed a piano was on fire.

Nangtong, appearance-emptiness. Dizziness.

Aung San Suu Kyi, peaceful Buddhist versus brutal military in Burma.

Diffuse cloud of smoke to the north. But you have your own bad news, don't you? OR doesn't pay attention to the news; to him it's all samsara, beings subject to the 3 poisons going round & round, living & dying, going through the bardos... His bodhicitta covers it all...

The violin concerto again. I like how the melody comes & goes, the sweet bird of the instrument in the hands of Hilary Hahn. And the orchestra...

Aaron's grandmother died; may she have a joyful rebirth. I'll mention her in the "Prayer for Extreme Times."

Nick records my 5 William Blake songs, plus "Easy Listening." Also gets me on bandcamp.com. We may go to Taos so Shanny can be in the video. I wait to hear from her but now she's grieving...

Center for Biological Diversity: a federal judge just ruled that polar bears must stay protected under the Endangered Species Act. Pacheco fire is 10k acres, 55%. Las Conchas fire at 113k, 6%. NASA Earth Observatory photo: brown desert, dark green mountains, white pattern of clouds, gray smoke blowing north.

Marie, do you have a boyfriend? I mean, do you want to go out for tea sometime? Maybe you could record one of my songs...

NPR: Ghaddafi threatens EU; EU $17 billion to Greece; 3 dead in Mexico City from Tropical Storm Arlene's record rainfall. ABC: 90s & 100s all over the south. Some rain in Los Alamos. I watch *Masterpiece Theater's Little Dorritt* by Dickens; read about Guru Rinpoche.

July 3

21 prostrations. Focus on the unfocused. Delay my Cymbalta till after breakfast to see if I'll be less dizzy during *ngondro*. "Dizzy Miss Lizzy."

Superficial news doesn't look at the underlying causes of fires, of polar bear distress, of samsara. But I can't help listening. The causes: poisonous negative emotions are increasing. The ignorance inherent in technology... May virtue increase!

Go to Copper Mountain. It's a study group session with Jane speaking on our lineage. She's nervous & has trouble pronouncing the Tibetan names. But she says something good she learned: that relationship with teacher is necessary for enlightenment. (I wish I was with OR & he was speaking on the lineage.) Lots of mentions of charnel grounds & miracles. Vimalamitra rode a blue elephant. The girls are awed but I voice skepticism. Buddha himself said we should be skeptical. But I do believe in APR's miracles... Corey mentions a dream she had of being dead & unable to communicate to the living.

Daniel finds a fledgling under his truck. What to do? Carol brings out a little cardboard box. There are too many cats around so I take the poor bird to Rio Grande Nature Center. It's named #1033 but not identified. It has a yellow-tipped tail & red tips on its wings. I'll call later to see what it is. Pamphlet says only 30% of all babies born in the wild survive their first year. Big beautiful thunder clouds are brewing in the atmosphere.

I'm still wondering what to do, where to live, who to love, whether to go to the *nyungne* retreat. I call Helen. And talk myself into going with her to the retreat. I figure if she can do it so can I, in spite of my attachments to food, sleep & the world of my ego. We will drive to Denver on the 21st & stay in Rinpoche's basement for one night before going up to the mountains.

But I'm still worried. If only I weren't bipolar. Of course, I will take my medications. I watch a DVD, *Barney's Version*, half-believable samsaric drama with Paul Giamatti & Rosamund Pike, goddess.

116

July 4

Dream of Amma's presence. Don't want to wake up.

FB: magic mushrooms are being used for terminally ill patients to give them a spiritual experience. I never took mushrooms, only LSD & grass. My faith now is in magic people.

Inciweb: Lab will reopen to employees on July 6. Cause of fire: fallen tree, power line. 123k, 19%. Desert walk in the neighborhood but don't buy the paper. Ad on youtube: see how polar bears are seeking fun in the sun with Pepsi. You gotta be kidding me! Talk about being cut off from nature, from reality.

I google endangered species of New Mexico. According to the state, 5 hummingbirds are threatened. 122 species are threatened or endangered: 25 fish, 6 amphibians, 15 reptiles, 33 birds, 16 mammals, 25 mollusks, 2 crustaceans. Just to name a few that are endangered (the most at risk), there are the Rio Grande silvery minnow, the Jemez Mountain salamander, the sand dune lizard, the aplomado falcon & the white-tailed ptarmigan. The pika isn't listed; nor the Mexican spotted owl. But Wild Earth Guardians, in May of this year, entered into an historic settlement with the US Fish & Wildlife Service to change the way that species are listed as threatened or endangered. One fifth of world mammals are threatened...

#1033 is a cedar waxwing! Not common around here the message says. I look it up; ah yes, the tail is dipped in yellow paint like a paintbrush!

"May it be that I & all limitless sentient beings, in all of our lifetimes, come into contact with authentic mentors—friends in virtue who will show us the path." —APR.

Sue calls. It's wet there in FL; they've had rain. She went swimming in the Gulf, saw a swallow-tailed kite last week. She was depressed by the non-virtue of others...Neighbor Tom has a big tumor...

Climate Progress (Joseph Romm): The Declaration of Interdependence—"It is the laws of Nature, studied & enumerated by scientists, that make clear we are poised to render those unalienable rights all but unattainable for billions of humans on our current path of unrestricted GHG emissions."

Yes, we need a miracle. We need to all practice wise compassion...

Hardly any fireworks around the neighborhood. Only limited types were legal this year & the governor put out the word that it would be unpatriotic to light fireworks in the middle of a hot, dry fire season. So I get right to sleep at 9.

Chapter 9
Caught Up

July 5

Dream of walking & swimming in beautiful water off Terra Ceia. Mangroves, seaweed, homes right on the water. Feeling of joy & freedom. Another dream: a girl who hated me at an empowerment.

Earthweek: A Diary of the Planet (earthweek.com). Bill Patzert, NASA climatologist, says La Nina quickly disappeared in January & turned into La Nada. Jet stream went nuts, leading to polar outbreaks such as we had here. I was wondering how the cool waters of La Nina could come about with the oceans warming. Anyway, they suddenly went away. Also, Arctic melting is resulting in species migration from the Pacific to the Atlantic. Gray whales & plankton not seen before. Horn of Africa suffering from horrific drought & famine. High for the week, Mecca, 118; low, Vostok, Antarctica, minus 105.

Should I move to Florida in November? Or should I go back to the cab? Money matters. I don't want to burden my siblings or daughter when I'm older.

I go to the dentist for cleaning & X-rays. Back home for peanut butter & jelly & an hour nap. I decide to go down to 50 mg. of trazadone for a week. 100 mg. making me too sleepy & dizzy I think. Doctor says I can experiment with that pill; it's mainly for sleeping better.

It's really hot out. I drive to the library & pick out 5 publishers from the *Songwriters' Directory*. Back home, feeling hopeful, I hear a knock on the door. "Will Humans Ruin This Earth?" It's a Jehovah's Witness flyer. Daniel had a dream 2500 years ago that explains everything. Big doings at the big Santa Ana Center. "God's Kingdom Will Crush All Other Kingdoms—When?"

More mantras. Then watch Michelle Pfeiffer in *The Fabulous Baker Boys*. Great singer & so sexy.

Trazodone, 50 mg.

July 6

I sleep differently, not so sleepy. And not so dizzy during practice.

OR on YouTube: "It's important to know things are empty…"

I call Susan, the woman from the CID hearing whose # is in the Sierra Club newsletter. Sort of in my age group; I liked her. She's showing DVD on fracking, says to email her because she's in the middle of something. Nice emails, wants to meet after she is back in town. Strictly business.

Las Conchas fire 131k, 30%, 2557 personnel. Pacheco fire 10k, 60%.

I remember to watch *Dinosaur Train*. Cute baby pterodons or whatever. Tiny, Shiny & Buddy. Family values. Dr. Scott, the paleontologist says "get outside, get into nature & make your own discoveries." Watch some *Sesame Street* too. May the innocent children be happy...

Call Nick, go to bank to see when I can cash out my IRA. Oct. 7.

CP: "Another power station was shut down by jellyfish today amid claims that climate change is causing a population surge among the species." Ouch. Acidification is leading to less shelled animals which is causing more gelatinous species... But the cost of solar is coming down fast. But they are using Agent Orange to clear forest in the Amazon. Sadness over FOX News distortions, the famine in Africa, jellyfish.

"May whatever I do, with body, speech or mind, bring nothing but benefit to all sentient beings, my very own parents." —Jigme Lingpa.

It's the Dalai Lama's birthday, age 76. Free Tibet! But someone on FB says he's a fraud for eating meat... If I was a cow, I would want to have a connection to the Dalai Lama. But it is hard to understand for militant vegetarians (& for me).

Local news at 6: a bear had burns from the Las Conchas fire & had to be put down.

Facebook Lora is sad about the earth. I comment "compassion needs to be balanced by the wisdom that it's all a dream."

I make some notes for the upcoming video of "Precious Human Lifetime." Years after writing the song, I now know that there is a difference between a "mere" human life & a "precious" one. The difference is that a human who practices the dharma has a precious human life. But the song gets it right when it says "the truth, it's the only way."

FB: Nancy in Denver likes my CD I gave her. She is going to *nyungne*.

120

July 7

Nightmare of a woman I liked but with clinging, clawing cats & a totally weird dad & family. Of course, I'm naked & confused.

The Dalai Lama begins big Kalachakra empowerment in DC. Wheel of Time.

Looking for good news in the paper, looking for love somewhere. Good news is the temperature won't be over 95 for a while (but low of 72 is 8 above normal). Denver today: 86–61. Massive dust storm strikes Phoenix. I mile high & 100 miles wide "haboob" covers the city at 60 mph. What a mess! Obama becomes first president to tweet. FB adds Skype option. Google comes up with Google+.

I wonder how many mantras I could say in one day. What's my personal best? I think I'll top it today. Om Ah Hung Vajra Guru Padme Siddhi Hung!

And I am all caught up with my diary!

I could end it here! But I want to share with you OR, part 3 & a happy ending with a girlfriend & a major win in the battle against fossil fuels would be nice, say in August in DC, against the tar sands pipeline. What about the urgency? The sooner it's published, the more lives will be saved. I hope that's true.

Rick calls. He says Lake Champlain is already gone in terms of invasive species taking over. But Lake George, where he & Gloria will go soon, is in good shape because the residents there have money they are putting into controlling invaders like the zebra mussel. And San Francisco has an early warning system against invasive species. He's an amateur botanist. The DNA sequencing revolution is going to change the names of every plant he says… He advises me on my money. He had 30 cedar waxwings land in his apple tree once.

The locust tree way in the back toward the mountains, which I can't reach with the hose, is alive in the drought, the driest January–June half-year in history in NM.

If I didn't play music, if I didn't listen to the news, I could complete my guru yoga more quickly. If I didn't write or look out the window or nap or have so many attachments… Imagine doing it in 3–6 months as APR recommends! Renunciation!

Las Conchas fire = 137k, 40% containment. It's 98 degrees downtown.

Astronauts talk about being in space: 250 miles up they could see Beijing fireworks once. BBC: Murdoch's *News of the World* shuts down due to its phone-hacking scandal. But Rupert still controls 40% of the media in UK. And Fox & the *Wall Street Journal* here.

Ananda emails the food requirements for sharing at *nyungne*. I'm to bring salad, dressing, nuts & a bottle of fruit juice for each of two days. About 20 to attend. Angela B. not coming.

I watch Michelle Pfeiffer again, as aging courtesan in *Cherie*.

July 8, Friday

I dream that I'm in a huge hotel/mall where Amma has been, looking for room 201 where a mass is to be held. Elevator, big wheels, way up high, I finally find the room at the top but there's nobody there. I rest as young dancers go by. The Wheel of Life is a Tibetan image portraying the 6 realms of existence one could be born into. What's the highest one could get in samsara? LSD, as Trungpa Rinpoche said once? Sex?

I get into YouTube for a while. Sexiness & humor. Why go get guitar strings? I will do another partial retreat & extra mantras. I volunteered to present a discussion of Guru Rinpoche to Copper Mountain. Maybe I'll compare him to Jesus. Both had miraculous births & deaths. Even if that's not true, they were considered so accomplished that the stories were told. Jesus was killed by dualistic thinking of the Jewish & Roman powers that be. Guru Rinpoche was killed by dualistic thinking too but kept resurrecting. In the end, they both just floated off. But the "Second Buddha" (as the Tibetans called Guru Rinpoche) left behind many accomplished students to carry on his lineage.

Spricket24 says I should fall in love with someone just one grade different than I am. What am I, a 5? Well, now I'm 67, maybe only a 4 or a 3…Is Susan a 6? Tasha? Nancy? R. definitely a 9; no wonder she changed her mind about me. It's a bubble-headed way of thinking but it makes sense in terms of people's attachments. In other words, get real.

"May all beings have happiness & the cause of happiness. May they be free of suffering & the cause of suffering. May they never be separate from true happiness free from suffering. May they abide in great equanimity, free from partiality & prejudice towards self & others." The prayer of the 4 immeasurables. From the Medicine Buddha text.

Death comes closer every day. Om tare tutare ture soha. I get *Guru Rinpoche: His Life & Times* off the shelf of books that Ismael left with me.

BBC: new country, #193, South Sudan, faces war & drought. Ten million at risk in East Africa from drought, civil war. Libya, Syria fighting.. Egyptian demonstrations over slow pace of change. Last Space Shuttle launches. Local: monsoons coming Monday & Tuesday? PBS: Exxon-Mobil 42,000 gallon spill in Yellowstone River. 8,000 miles of pipelines in Montana. Big snowmelt runoff. Keystone XL pipeline would cross the river too.

Personal best; solitude all day.

July 9

Lots of dreams about faces eaten away, including old friend Lin who won't look at me. Wake, dream, wake dream. Came home to Wolfgang's & gas was on high, Chris sleeping, little Shannon playing with art words. A horse running at us: I hold up incense to pacify it. Shanny wanted French toast.

Awake.

Chris Hedges writes that he will protest October 6. What about August 6?

Nick helps me for 2 hours; I get new guitar strings put on by Ian. Cate wants to go to Copper Mountain tomorrow. Shannon replies, so we will go to Taos for "Precious Human Lifetime" soon, not sure what day yet. She's going to Chicago July 21, two days after her birthday.

5, 97 degrees. Las Conchas fire at 140k, 40%. Superficial news. Prostration time. Mozart for dinner as I look out window at doves & jets. I thought it was raining for a minute. It was that hallucination I have when I think it is raining. Now it's time for *Little Dorrit*.

July 10

It's my parents' wedding day, my conception day.

Dream of view from high up on cliff of farms, a horse, a river. Like the view from near Cabezon Peak where I last camped out with Rick & Gloria. Or the view from the petroglyphs near La Cienega. Also, cleaning up a little kid's shit at a Rainbow Gathering, I'm excited that someone has a shovel.

Heart Essence of the Vast Expanse. Do it again, until I reach enlightenment for the true happiness of everyone. It has to start with me & I see I need help. So I take refuge in the awakened ones. Since the Big Bang, all beings connected. Then, raise bodhicitta, purify obscurations, offer mandala & body, merge mind with guru mind. All beings doing it with me. I'm a slow learner, but I have excellent teachers.

Republicans are on an ideological crusade to repeal energy standards for lightbulbs! "It is dangerous for the press to hammer away at the theme that antidepressants are placebos. They're not. To give the impression that they are is to cause needless suffering." —Peter D. Kramer in NYT.

Lama Tsultrim says today's Guru Rinpoche day is especially powerful. Om ah hung vajra guru padme siddhi hung.

9:30, wait for Cate, Tara in disguise. 9:39, patience time. I call: she thought I wrote be here at 10.

*   *   *

Just back from Copper Mountain. Cate has accused me & every man she's ever met of being perverse. Oh, it's not that bad. I've agreed to water now only once a week but for an hour on the wisteria. She knows a lot about wisteria. It would have been better to be patient, but I wasn't. Meat-eating discussion during the Tara tsok. David & Carol et al look for loopholes in APR's no-meat vows. I get a bit assertive that he highly recommends vegetarian diet, thinking that people always just think they need to eat meat. Look at India, entirely vegetarian. Look at APR!

Cate emails proof that I said be here at 10. My bad again!

Time for phowa practice at Helen & Michael's. Scattered showers on the way home. .18 inch at Wyoming & Indian School; nothing here but gutters run.

60 Minutes: Twice the amount of Saudi oil here in the US in natural gas. "Shaleionaires" get rich from fracking under their homes. Chesapeake Energy honcho says that natural gas emits half the CO_2 as coal. Sierra Club's Michael Brune thinks gas is OK as long as there are rules on the fracking chemicals getting in the water. I wonder what Susan thinks.

July 11

What is a dream? Memory & imagination arising in awareness when the senses are shut down. Illusion.

Scientist in *NY Times* pushes for expensive fusion. One third of adults suffer chronic pain. (I'm lucky) Interstate Stream Commission is pumping ground water into the Pecos River to meet needs downstream in Carlsbad. Om tare tutare ture soha. Inciweb: Flash flood watch now in effect through Tuesday evening. Las Conchas, 147,642; 50%. Pacheco, 10k, 65%.

I turn water on the wisteria before my walk, let it go an hour. After, lazy, I lie down to listen to Thom Hartmann. He fears the Republicans want to win at any cost, including destroying the economy. Maybe there should be a primary challenge to Obama from the left.

Don't be fooled by samsara; be mindful of attachments. I get up & meditate.

#1033 is doing great. He's self-feeding now & will be released in the East Mountains. A rehabber out there has a lot of cedar waxwings in his yard.

Noticing my energy yesterday. There's a thin line between love & hate. So much liking & disliking. At least, I'm sort of mindful of it as it comes up.

"The numbers are staggering: tar sands mining in Canada's Boreal forest could claim the lives of 160 million migratory birds—including millions of backyard songbirds we love seeing & hearing every summer." —NRDC.

Big nap. Sue calls: she had to take old Jim to the doctor but he's OK. Mosquito helicopter going over as we speak. I talk briefly of not wanting to go back to work Aug. 8. Is it just a concept or do I need more time for book & music? Or am I just too tired & old?

Inside Job DVD by Charles Ferguson. I think it won an Oscar for best documentary. It starts in Iceland in 2000. Somehow businesses were deregulated & the three largest banks were privatized & started loaning money they didn't have. Alcoa built geothermal smelters for aluminum, destroyed land. In spite of their democracy, a few high-rollers ruined the economy. The same thing happened in US. Reagan deregulated financial sector. Those who refused to be interviewed for the film: Greenspan, Summers, Goldman Sachs CEOs, ratings agencies, Paulson, Laura

Tyson, presidents of Harvard & Columbia, Geithner, Bernanke. Greed & corruption fueled ideology. Short-term profits, fraud, lying. Economy crashes. $700 billion bailout under Bush. And now, the banks are bigger than ever. Financial sector lobbies & contributes to campaigns & controls the business schools. Obama nominates Geithner as Treasury Secretary, Summers as advisor. Eliot Spitzer is critical of them. Maybe he should run for president.

July 12

Dreamed I was a wandering hippie like the old me, with a broken backpack, looking for a place to sleep. Also, woke up from sleeping in car with Dad, in Seattle. I could see the Space Needle through binoculars...

NY Times: milkweed habitat for Monarch butterfly decimated by Roundup herbicide on genetically modified crops. 94% of the soybeans, 72% of the corn are GMOs in the US. Drought in TX kills 30% of the wheat; price of beef to go down as ranchers sell off herds, then way up as supply shrinks. No mention of fossil fuel addiction.

CP: Al Gore planning "24 Hours of Reality," live from every time zone, Sept. 14–15. He changed name from Alliance for Climate Protection to the Climate Reality Project to emphasize the current reality of global warming. Republicans seek to slash funding for clean energy, Democrats want to shift funds from fossil fuels to renewables. NY Times asks why "horrible" US drought "has come on extra hot & extra heavy." Their answer is...La Niña, of course!

Still waiting for promised rain here. Earthweek.com: 121 F. in East Mesa, AZ; minus 97 F. at South Pole. NOAA says every US state is now warmer on average than it was 30 years ago. Earthweek links to Al Gore's new video.

New Mexicans are suing governor over energy efficiency rules being overturned.

Tar sands: 4 tons of earth moved for a single barrel of oil. Area the size of North Carolina in NE Alberta. "The boreal forest as we know it could be gone in a generation without major policy changes." —Steve Kallick, Pew Boreal Campaign.

208 days in Albuquerque with .10 inches or less rain. NBC, 24 states & 124 million people under a heat advisory. 102 in St. Louis. What

explains it? The weather channel guy says the jet stream. What about global warming? PBS: heat wave story leads, but first: a lie from Chevron.

A beautiful evening for a walk as I yawn. Western clouds have cooled the air & there's a nice breeze. I take my pills at 8; I wonder how late Susan stays up.

July 13

Dreamed I was on a fire-escape-like ladder way up high at a basketball game & when it was over (Shannon 104, someone else 103) (but it wasn't quite over), a guy pulled a lever & I went down in a rollercoaster-like car, down into a swimming pool. I got out of the pool & befriended an upset black toddler boy named Miriam. Something about "Dog Is Love" bumpersticker I saw yesterday.

Research the 8 manifestations of Guru Rinpoche.

Then TH: Supreme Court has become a monarch to veto laws such as McCain–Feingold campaign finance reform & increase corruption. Obama should empanel a grand jury to investigate Clarence Thomas & Antonin Scalia.

One hour of guru yoga = 2000 mantras.

USA Today: "More than 100 environmental activists from across the country descended Tuesday on the Montana Capitol to demand Gov. Brian Schweitzer rescind his support for the Keystone XL oil pipeline & Exxon-Mobil's megaload transportation project." The governor is a Democrat who says he's for clean energy.

Nyungne email. Angela T. is the same as Angela B! Expect heavy rain.

Radio-mozart. Wow! I call Helen. She's working on OR's new book, Journey to Certainty or some such title. She reads final draft to him over Skype. We discuss nyungne details.

CP: GOP's Dirty Bulb Bill Burns Out—failed to pass the House; Cleantech Jobs Reach 2.7 million.

I need a rest at 1:30.

Get up & write with tired eyes. Should I stop trazodone completely? Three hours to Susan. "Nowhere Man" in E. Just be yourself no matter what they say. Every angel is terrible. But when I find the room for Gasland, Susan is not here. Ah, here she is: I stare at her but shake myself out of it. I reintroduce myself; she has a certain beauty,

127

no doubt about it. She takes charge of the meeting & gets right to showing the movie. Josh Fox gets an offer of $100,000 to drill his acres in Pennsylvania. But after he finds out that there are 596 chemicals in the hydraulic fracturing fluid & starts investigating with his camera, he refuses to sign. The water is polluted with people sick in Dimock. There is no oversight of the natural gas industry because of Dick Cheney's influence, the "Halliburton loophole." Turn on the water faucet & light it up. Methane escaping into the atmosphere along with volatile organics that cause neurological damage. Josh goes west & discovers "gasland" is everywhere: TX, CO & north.

She's cute but I can't make a move & come home tired. Could I still call her? Yes, but...

Zero trazodone.

July 14

Dream that I'm at the stupa. There's another half stupa there too, to be put up nearby. I tell someone that I dream about the stupa.

Intermittent sleep mixed with the new Tara chant. Susan keeps popping up in my morning meditations. I'm half ready for a new song to come but rational mind says to call first before writing another foolish love song.

NY Times: American Electric Power has decided to table plans to build a full-scale carbon-capture plant at Mountaineer, a 31-year-old coal-fired plant in West Virginia, where the company has successfully captured & buried CO_2 in a small pilot program for 2 years.

Gasland—what a devastating movie. The gas business intentionally making people & animals sick & then lying about it. And T.Boone Pickens' NAT GAS Act is just to expand production of this polluting fossil-fuel & make him billions of dollars more. Natural gas is not clean & the bureaucrats have no moral spine...

I decide to email Susan instead of calling. I ask how many times she's seen the movie, what's going on in Mora fracking situation. I tell her a bit about this book: "If any of this interests you, maybe we could have lunch sometime & talk." Send.

Richmond VA low was 81 degrees on July 12, breaking record high minimum temperature by 5 degrees.

FB, Costanzo Allione: "I'm about to meet the Karmapa for the first time." Foodandwaterwatch.org.

Factory farm map & charts. Over a billion broilers in the US; 10 million cattle. In NM, 1 factory farm dairy cow per 6 people. Massive overwhelm. Om tare tutare ture soha. Amma Amma Konachi. Peanut butter & jelly for lunch.

I start reading the novel *Returning to Earth* by Jim Harrison. Sue gave it to me.

Leisure! Thanks to a human life (1944–) in the US, a chance to understand, enjoy & practice. Day after day, alone on a hill... Walk to apartments & back as nice sunset lines up. No reply from Susan.

50 mg traz.

July 15

Dream: a line of us following OR through forest in mountains, woodcutters off to the side. We carry firewood. I get off path going around a stump & struggle to climb back up to it. It would have been better to retrace my steps.

"Don't prolong the past, don't invite the future..."

Susan replies: movie showing in Santa Fe Saturday with Mora people. Gaslandthemovie.com. She's probably in a relationship...

NY Times: New Herbicide Suspected in Tree Deaths (DuPont's Imprelis). Paul Krugman, "Getting to Crazy"—Commentators seem shocked at Republican unreasonableness as a debt default looms, but it is the end result of a process that has lasted decades...

Center for Biological Diversity: Landmark Agreement Pushes 757 Species Toward Protection. 41pounds.org stops junk mail. Eliza Gilkyson research & listening. Will I go hear her tonight? Alone? "At the end of a golden age..." "Highway." Red House Records.

Another hot, dry day. But there's a new cloud in the sky: it's a pyrocumulus, up Jemez way. I go to InciWeb but it's not on there yet. Las Conchas is 150k, 61%, 1001 sweating personnel. I'm tired, so lie down with Randi on the radio. She's excited that Murdoch's empire is crumbling.

CP: "Extremist climate science deniers like Michelle Bachman & Tim Pawlenty are campaigning tirelessly to give their state the climate of Texas." "Back in mid-April, only 10% of TX was under exceptional drought. Now a staggering 71% is!" While concerns over fracking grow—4 PA summer camps to host drilling operations.

Text from Shan: she has a meeting at 2 tomorrow so Nick & I will have to leave earlier & hustle. She wants me to bring her friend Miriam up too.

Live at 5: no new fire; it is back-burning of Las Conchas fire in gusty winds. 3.81 normal rain usually; .19 actual. Why, Byron Morton, weatherman? ABC: Murdoch says he's sorry. 160 people died of heat last year in the US. Endangered species chocolate for desert: cacao grown in the natural shade of rich, diverse forests. 10% of net profits donated to help support species, habitat & humanity. I'm eating the Sea Turtle variety, dark chocolate with blueberries.

Drillingmoracounty.blogspot.com. Extinctioncrisis.org: 7 billion humans in 3 months.

After I go to bed, my dear daughter calls with directions to Miriam's apartment. Then I can't get to sleep, thinking about the video we are about to make & the trip to Taos...

July 16

Slept badly. Clinging kittens, cab, Cate, running out of food. Dispel obstacles! Oh, man... I buy gas & Adrenal Health capsules which include Rhodiola & Holy Basil (tulsi, Amma's favorite). Pick up Nick & Miriam & off we go. We see smoke from the fire, south of Tent Rocks. Nick burned me 2 CDs! (Talking Heads & Elvis Costello). Miriam's work involves 2 different projects: looking for a fungus that will decompose cellulose at high temperatures for biofuels & researching the fungus that the pine bark beetle carries which kills trees. A biologist at work. We listen to *Fear of Music*.

We meet Shannon at a coffee place where her former boyfriend now works. We find a place with a beautiful view of the gorge & proceed to lip-synch badly. I can't hear the cheap boombox on the first take & get off beat. Second take: Shanny wears the purple, feathery mask that's been hanging in her room forever. We're better, because I'm just faking the chords. My song "Precious Human Lifetime" coming out of my ears still. Third take is with Shannon, my back-up singer, shining her flashlight when I sing "let me see your light shine..." She gives me a kiss & we go back to Taos. She & Mir go to movie with her friend Mirabai in it. Nick & I eat at the park. I take two more Adrenal Health pills & we have a quiet trip home. I pay Nick 5 twenties signed by Timothy Geithner. Was it all worth it?

July 17

Papagena! Papageno! Mozart radio. After Guru Rinpoche of course.

Gretchen, Jane, Corey, Geraldine, Carol & Bernie are present for my talk on the life of Guru Rinpoche at Copper Mountain. Ego present too. Or is it divine pride? Do Vajrasattva mantra anyway. Talk to Bernie a little.

Peanut butter & jelly on way to stupa in Santa Fe. I circumambulate in the wind the gleaming white dream-mind of the Buddha temple doing mantras. Then visit Norma. She saw *The Tree of Life*, wants me to call her after I see it… I meet Lama Mingma & good old Lama Dorje tells the same old jokes as we eat left-overs from the full moon feast. Lama Mingma catches a prairie dog & holds it up by the back leg.

Then, with Chris to *The Tree of Life*. Beautiful tears at the preciousness of life, human flaws… Chris not so impressed. We're still in the slow movie out in the sun again. Is it all a dream?

Back to Hopi Street, where Chris picks me some lettuce from his luxuriant garden; Christine heats up lentils. It's fine weather to eat out back at sundown. They are going to Paris in a week. The hour drive home is with Elvis Costello.

July 18

What a movie! *The Tree of Life*.

Low 74, 9 above normal. Gold over $1600; Dow down 180. TH: Republicans' win-at-any-cost tricks/sabotage/treason in Nixon, Reagan, Bush victories. Will there be an October surprise next year? Prophecy from Guru Rinpoche in *The Legend of the Great Stupa*: "corrupt & selfish men become leaders…drunkards preach the path to salvation…plagues, famines & war…"

Many thoughts, therefore many spaces between thoughts!

100/64 is my blood pressure; 96.6, my body temperature; 178, my weight. I'm at the clinic, waiting to see Dr. Gibson for annual check-up. Then, Jon, for the last time. He says I'd be a good candidate for meds only (no counseling needed) so I go for it. I'm a little sad but he's not a very good counselor anyway. One less person in my life.

Home to nap, then call Sue. She thinks I should work for 6 months! I'm not so sure.

July 19

Dream of not taking acid while others do; fire, camping, losing my favorite, stainless steel Sierra cup.

It's Shannon's birthday. She's 24.

NY Times: "...the weather forecast has become about saving lives." "The UN should affirm that if an island nation loses its permanent population & territory to rising seawater, the world will continue to recognize its sovereignty as a nation." President of Nauru, an eight square mile nation in the Pacific, thinks he has a chance. I don't think so.

Well, I could use the money, to support dharma & writing. Go back to cab in October? Samsara, my money...

To Nick's where I suggest edits to the video. He puts the Wheel of Life picture at the beginning & Guru Rinpoche picture at the end. The lip-synching doesn't matter much because there are no close-ups. It turns out pretty good! And he only charges me another $50.

CP: Did News Corp hack the "climategate" emails to try to make a scandal out of climate science? An Oil Spill Runs Through It: Montana Suffers Another Pipeline Rupture. Led by Murdoch Outlets, Conservative Media Misled Light Bulb Consumers 40 Times in 7 Months.

Wow, Rupert Murdoch's trophy wife is hot! He's 80; she's young. She gives a right hook to a would-be pie-in-the-face thrower! Talking heads on the news say the billionaire did a good job of testifying before a parliamentary committee. But how about systematic lying to the public through his media outlets? Bad karma, Murdoch. There is also radioactive beef from Fukushima area; and the f-word, famine, in East Africa, is officially declared. Heat wave in US. 126 degrees in Newton, Iowa? 126? That's got to be wrong...

July 20

I dream of eating a bite of wild fig from a vine on a tall tree, then sharing it.

132

I just drink tea with no milk. Fasting for blood work at 9. The prayer flags are calm. Am I too dizzy to drive cab again? I think like that when meditating in the morning. Too tired…Too old…And there are more important things to do…On this date in 1969, Neil Armstrong became the first man to walk on the moon. I was doing LSD with Chris Garrison.

Draw blood as Bernie calls. I meet him at "Starlight" (he means "Satellite"). He's 72. His twin sister & older, autistic brother are his responsibility. They are the last of 10 children. On Sunday, he finished his 100,000 prostrations for *ngondro*. Now he needs to do the mandala offering he says. He mentions that an AA friend of his is looking for a temporary room to rent. Kevin works at Sandia Lab, is getting divorced & letting his wife live in their house for now.

Just watched "Precious Human Lifetime" on YouTube. Check it out! Very nice. "Ah" comes up next but "One Earth, One Sky" is on 350.org account I guess. "Mi lu Rinpoche" (Tibetan for precious human life) links to "Rangzen Walk Mi Mang Lang Lu" & "Tibetan Uprising Song."

Kevin calls; Bernie is his sponsor. Maybe this could work out & I could save $300 a month or so.

CP: Mozambique Cuts Poverty, Creates Jobs with Clean Energy. The Arctic's death spiral continues.

Caught up again. Get ready for OR3, dear reader. A retreat in the Rockies. No CP, no *NYTimes*. No FB or email. No phone. Nothing but love…

Arctic death spiral. The paper says high in Des Moines yesterday was 98. That 126 was the heat index, which figures in humidity. Good interview with the Dalai Lama on candle4tibet.org. He says his next life is up to himself only, not China. That would apply to all of us.

Kevin comes by but doesn't stay long. He'll think it over. He has no kids.

6:21, we interrupt this weather forecast with the sound of raindrops, right here on Jefferson St.! I watch out the east window: beautiful rain, moistening the dirt & roots & leaves. At last. Norma calls. We discuss the movie. Still raining; gutter flowing. A note from a music publisher: sorry.

USA Today: 17 states hit the 100 degree mark; more than 40 states over 90 degrees.

Chapter 10
OR3

Dreamed I smoked pot but regretted it. I drink grape juice before *ngondro*; not so dizzy.

Times: Climate Change Security Council Talks Deadlock, also: Seeing Trends, Coalition Works to Help a River Adapt (the Nisqually River, between Mount Rainier & Puget Sound).

Now, here, this body, speech & mind is the perfect place to be, to start to be, from which to start a journey. Hung hung hung! Helen will be here in 20 minutes. Play a bit. An old song of mine, "Falling in Love with the Earth."

And off we go. No fire smoke; lots of humidity. Michael is in Paris visiting his two daughters who live in Germany. Helen says OR's health is OK. His birthday is in May. He's 42; Melissa, 37. We stop at Real Food Nation in Eldorado. Veggies grow outside; boys play. I packed a peanut butter & jelly sandwich so I just get pomegranate-green tea to go. Helen gets eggs. Give her my CD & we put it on. "The Sun Will Rise," "let me feel your love-mind." Blue & white planet; Mora County.

Feel queasy, maybe from the tea with no milk or maybe the motion of the car. I ask to stop in Maxwell for a breather. A one horse town. Then I drive to the rest stop north of Trinidad where I finally eat my sandwich. Rain, glorious rain. Stop in Colorado Springs for Reed's ginger ale & petrol. Helen's Kia Optima is getting 35 mph. Double rainbow.

OR to give Green Tara empowerment in late October in Santa Fe. Greenland, Colorado. I wonder how summer is going on the ice of the big Greenland. Then Denver. Where to eat dinner? BOA's: foxy waitress with broken fingers & a "Ski Naked" T-shirt. I take a long time eating my nachos delicioso. Helen can't eat much. Then to OR's house. Melissa seems stressed; Rinpoche walking the dog. Helen shows me the basement shrine room where I have a nice electric air mattress. At 9 I take my pills.

In the bathroom: The true meaning of life: "We are visitors on this planet. We are here for ninety or 100 years at the very most. During that period, we must try to do something good, something useful, with our lives. If you contribute to other people's happiness, you will find the true goal, the true meaning of life." —His Holiness the 14th Dalai Lama

July 22

Three of us men go to Danny DeVito movie & all sleep through it. Dream.

Helen is in constant backpain. Once involved with Swami Satchitananda, Lakota & Pima medicine men. Now she is the secretary to OKL & OR. He comes in the room to get something as I do my guru yoga. Nice.

After shower & eggs I realize how tired I am. They were up till 10:30 talking about the new center, closing, insurance. And all but Helen were up again at 5 to practice. The clock ticked all night. I rest in the backyard with squirrels & flickers. Helen & Rinpoche on the computer.

I walk around the block; it's humid here. Squirrels, pigeons & crows eat together from grain someone offered them in the street. Then I hang out in basement, not wanting to interfere with the meeting upstairs. Rinpoche on phone now; he has learned English so well in 5 years. I'm cooling down. What to do? I'm a bit lonely.

Then lunch at Pho Fusion with the man & his secretary. I'm starstruck.

4:30, my new bed for 8 nights in cabin 3. Aspens out the window, so quiet. We bought food at Sunflower Market & drove up here to Jenka & Bob's retreat center near Mount Evans. 9800 feet. The gas we burn to get out of the heat & city...

Melody (Jenka's daughter) & husband & young son are just moving out. She went to see Amma with Easter & me when she was pregnant! (the last time I saw Easter) Helen & I are the first to arrive. Then comes Myra who puts up a big tent in an aspen grove. She asks me if the three-leaved plants are poison ivy! (they're strawberries) Check out the vacant yurt, hot in the sun. Then Nancy arrives, followed by John, my cabin mate. Helen can't believe it! Her bag of yogurt & cheese was left behind at Sunflower...

Pamphlet: *Ursus americanus*, average male 275 pounds, hibernates in winter. You can't outrun one.

John works at Naropa, has a portable cardboard shrine that's very elegant. Another John, from Qatar! (British) Rinpoche gives a short talk

136

in the yurt to those assembled after setting up the shrine, then he & his wife do chöd practice. I'm attached to sleep, stumble into cabin in the dark.

July 23

Sleep badly. I can't believe how warm it is. Cabin must be well insulated; my sleeping bag way too hot. Couldn't open window in the middle of the night. Dream of a drug-possessed human demon guy. I guess I have compassion for him because he finally lets go of me. I'm in my old truck at a barn like Greg's in Vermont. Where's the stupa? It was moved… I would have slept better with only a sheet. There's my 5 am alarm; there's the old moon…

John is packing up, has to go. He got a call from Naropa & everything there is falling apart. He wishes me a good *nyungne*.

We're supposed to wash our head, hands & feet so I shower quickly & walk up through the dark aspens to the yurt. Tom silently greets me with the ritual purification water which I swish & spit out. Entering the yurt, at first I don't notice the lama in the dim light in his dark red robes. I prostrate three times & take my chair. 14 present, plus Rinpoche & Melissa.

Because he hasn't taken the purification water yet Rinpoche can talk. He speaks of the kinds of vows. *Nyungne* vows are temporary. We will renew every morning before sunrise for a week. The practice originated with a nun, Gelongma Palmo, who cured her leprosy through doing thousand-armed Avalokiteshvara (Chenrezi) & attained great realization. The root vows are no killing, stealing, sex, lying or drinking alcohol. The inner vows are to regret past negative behavior; the secret vows are to not grasp at virtue or non-virtue. We will do a middle *nyungne*, which means that there will be no talking except at our one meal a day at lunch. OR: most days we chase after pleasure, have a bias toward our loved ones & against strangers, speak without mindfulness, get tangled up in greed through our work… It is important to put aside these things now & then. In a year there are very few days for virtue…

We take the vows. Rinpoche & Melissa drink the water. We do the Meditation on the Great Compassionate One: Om Mani Padme Hung Hri… Sing the mantra, then silently do it.

At 7 we break. I go back to cabin & drink some hot water. Not drinking water, except at lunch, is the best practice but Rinpoche says it is

OK to drink. Sun coming through the aspens. My belly is calm; I hear a woman talking. I lie down until the 9:30 practice session.

Trembling light in the yurt; Myra reading *Words of My Perfect Teacher*. Rinpoche's root lama, Tsara Dharmakirti, photo on shrine. Thankas hang on the yurt's walls: Guru Rinpoche, Vajrasattva, 1000-armed Chenrezi & 2 Green Taras. We chant, then sit silently. I glance at my fellow retreatants. Especially Tasha. Ananda & Leigh Ann are both married. An hour & a half goes by like the sun rising into the sky.

Lunch after washing out mouth. What to say now that I can talk? I sit on the floor between Leigh Ann & Rinpoche. Yapo du! Best meal ever, all vegetarian naturally. The courses just keep coming! I catch a flying bug & take it outside even though I'm not supposed to leave my seat. Fruit, chocolate. Too full. Tasha & others serve. She's married. Wash out mouth again & stop talking. I guess I'll walk. Oops, talked to myself!

Back to the yurt at 2:30: fluttering shadows as the earth turns in silence. We bow to Chenrezi. Manis turn into vajra guru mantra in my head once. Lack of mindfulness. Is Tina with Tom? Yawning sky as the afternoon heats up.

The fourth session is at 5:30. Getting into it. The mind that is.

7:28. No rain. I rejoice in our good fortune to be here together with OR, vajra master. I'll let the squirrel do the talking. I mistook the skylight crank in the yurt to be someone talking, the zippers on the windows to be Chris pissing on the deck. Tom's prayer wheel to be a circling insect! I need some sleep.

Elk in the meadow at sunset melt into a dream…

July 24

Sleep well with window open; dream of the bad old days with Shannon & her mom.

I don't take the vows since I'm serving today. I rejoice in others taking them though. Rinpoche explains that Gelongma Palmo practiced day & night, one pointedly. Yidam means bound to mind. Chenrezi is a yidam, an imagined deity for the mind to focus upon. We will experience difficulties & obscurations as we repair & purify our vows. Don't forget bodhicitta. The past is over; we can't change it. Don't worry about the future either. At least, try to have a balance between worldly & dharma. Then Melissa leads the Meditation on the Great Compassionate One: In the palace on the great holy mountain abides the speech emanation of the Buddhas, Avalokiteshvara, whose speech benefits beings above, below & throughout the ten directions… Om mani padme hung hri…

At break I'm sleepy after some Emergen-C. I eat the soymilk & cashews I brought. Then do some *ngondro* until Ananda knocks on the door encouraging me to come down to kitchen & help prep for lunch.

Four hours later I'm pooped. Prepped & served & cleaned. But I tried to carry too many plates & spilled food & coffee. Oh no! "This is bad, this is bad," I say, as Rinpoche hits me on the butt with a pillow & laughs. John from Qatar says it could happen to anybody. But I'm embarrassed. Chris says I guess you go back to Mindfulness 101…

2:30. Medicine Buddha, just what I need. But it's hard in the heat. Many doubts surface in my mind: are we a cult? Why didn't Rinpoche like the salad dressing? Attachment to self-esteem: there's a concept!

5:12, almost asleep. 18 minutes to practice. There should be wolves here…

July 25

Dream of a kiss. Who was it? Not SueShe. *Finnegans Wake* with my name in it.

I'm thirsty & I have a headache. A bird calls at 5:16. Austerity, joy, tea & ibuprofen before my next vows. The jungle comes alive with the sound of monkeys (crows). Old moon above the vertical aspens is the color of Chenrezi. Vow now, brown cow.

All of us are keeping the vows all day since it is tsok day & there is no food prep. *Nyungne* during this the sixth month of the Tibetan year is especially good. We should offer tsok with one pointedness. It took Asanga 12 years to establish his yidam. The time it takes depends on our obscurations. Tsok offering can lengthen one's life. Tsara Dharmakirti emphasized it & lived into his 90s.

When we start doing the beautiful Chenrezi mantra I cry.

Break. Wah-wah, I don't need no wah-wah… (George Harrison song in my head). Trying no water today. Walk out into the world of animals: duck in pond, fish, bugs, birds, somewhere elk, bear…

Beautiful tsok prayers & guru yoga in yurt. Then we move the food down to the Elk House for lunch. Lots of talk about the new center. Also talk of Steven Seagal, Ecstasy (the drug), healthy attachment

(Tasha talking). Plenty of wah-wah. Delicious food. Feel bloated. I lie down after my Cymbalta. Josh is moving into the cabin.

2:30. Looks like rain. Much cooler than yesterday afternoon. Waiting on Rinpoche. It's rain alright, & the 3 kayas...

When we leave yurt at 4, the rain has stopped so I walk up through the forest. Elk scratches on aspens. Spruce. Potentilla, paintbrush, white upside-down stars with green pistils. My brother would know the name I'll bet. Chairs up there by streams with simple bridges over them. Down around by Tina's tent, the main house to a hammock in the aspens. Elevation headache? Plus dehydration... It's like being on Sandia Crest.

Compassion for those in the sweltering lowlands, the heat-island cities. But at least they have oxygen. I'm going to ask Helen if we can go up to Mt. Evans on Saturday when we leave here.

4:58, time for the news (just kidding).

Aware space...

Dawn to dawn...

At the Doolittle Ranch. 12 bed, 8 bath, 5300 square feet, 147 acres, 40 acre meadow. $2.3 million. For sale.

5:30. Ananda always has a smile for me. Medicine Buddha for the thirsty & hungry, sick & dying, those sick of the three poisons...Then thigh-bone trumpets & damarus by Rinpoche & his wife.

July 26

Dream of Shannon doing an ultra-feminist barb-wire protest against oppression. (Tasha had said she believed that a woman needs a man like a fish needs a bicycle—until she met her husband) I wake up two times. Josh & I meet at the bathroom door & both of us say "go ahead" unmindfully.

Tina is lighting the butterlamps; Rinpoche helps make a wick. Melissa had to go back to work in the city.

1. Bodhicitta, tonglen, breathing, focus. "Giving & accepting." 2. Yidam visualization. 3. Reciting sadhana, mantra. 4. Rest in view, the yidam's mind. 21st century is the most afflicted environment. Reciting the mantra loudly gets rid of karmic wind. Then we do it silently; then rest. Rejoice in the path. When tired, remember the 21st century...

Time flies. A cup of Emergen-C, raspberry. Gray sky; big rest. Water is medicine, so I drink some.

Wild OR stories at lunch time. Magic. Lama Chupur getting stuck with a sword. A khenpo going up in a tornado & disappearing from Chinese custody. Rinpoche memorizing a text in his dreams. Tasha talking about touching. David S. & Nancy singled out as being single but no mention of my looking for a girlfriend. I chimed in that I had tried dharmamatch though. Talk to Tina a minute: she might teach at Naropa. Rinpoche teasing boys by pulling their "dorjes" when he was 17 & getting punished.

2:30, blue light special, healing this body & others with the 179-syllable mantra.

Later, just walked to the asphalt: all roads connected. BAU out there I suppose.

6:45. Rinpoche gets a good laugh out of Ananda having to take the torma offering out in the rain. Nancy & Tina go out to help with umbrella. Om mani padme hung hri. May the elements be in balance on earth. Hri.

7:44. Just down from yurt. We waited out the rain. Rinpoche so happy. Going back in room I think: oh, I did close the window. Oops, no I didn't. Edge of bed & books wet. I think Tim DeChristopher was sentenced today. Wonder what else happened. How about the debt ceiling? How about that Tina? I guess she & Tom aren't together.

July 27

Intense dream: I felt betrayed by parents. Confused emotions, guilt. I told my siblings I loved them. Norma too, who was walking with a crutch near a school. Where cops chased Bob, who was being chased by black guy about a camera. Wake at 1:48. I set a dead juniper on fire in the desert. There was a river with fox-like creatures snapping along in the current. Helen says all beings in dreams are the dreamer.

Angela shows up a minute late; we hadn't seen her since Friday night. Busy with nursing school I'm sure. Precious human life & perfect conditions to be here at *nyungne*, caring for each other. Impermanence: who knows what will happen next year or even the next day? The four mind turnings are equal to Vajrayana practice in importance. And remember how your visualization was when you first started; you are improving. Patience, diligence. Master one or two techniques. Even if you

141

die tomorrow, you have savings, you can remember your dharma practice. Sangha is precious.

In the palace on the great holy mountain...

After practice, everything outside is wet. A very gentle rain must have fallen; I didn't hear it. 7:14, back in bed after a drink. Some shortness of breath. 55 degrees in here. The heater isn't working but my sleeping bag is.

My parents were disappointed in me & were setting up a work schedule for me (busy work). I complained to Sue that I was writing a book & didn't want to do busy work. Some imp-like girl was on my side too.

8:26, after *ngondro*. I'm hungry! I fall asleep. Up at 9:29 & late for the yurt.

1:38, the opposite of hungry now. It's raining again. Tina wanted to talk but I had to run through the rain to the bathroom.

Parents = OR = me. Jesus is coming, look busy!

At lunch I asked Angela about the debt ceiling but she didn't want to talk politics. She said there are other Copper Mountains being built besides APR's.

There is the eco side of me & the Buddhist side. The first is worried about eco-cide; the second is into all is impermanent & mind is empty. The non-dual eco-Buddhist is where the compassion comes in. As the little yellow book says, "not to engage the mind in subject-object duality is the Bodhisattvas' practice" (#22).

Blue columbine, Steller's jay. Late again. I mistimed my walk & was way out past the meadow when I heard the gong. Out of breath for the first part of Medicine Buddha.

It's all flowing together. Big storm over the yurt: lightning bolts & thunder & lama laughing. A good place to die! Now it's 8. Josh just peed & brushed his teeth (but did he floss?) I'm ready too. Mind comes up with carrot & raisin salad idea for tomorrow.

July 28

Serving day. Dreamed of decadence, clubs, TV. I was helping a kid, looking for vegetarian food. Back to her parents' table: cops, someone was killed (her dad?). Samsara. I may have been eating a fish in tomato sauce.

5:30 am. Rinpoche not taking the vows today. He says faith & devotion can rid one of doubt & fear & neurosis. 98% of Tibetans aren't educated in Dharma but they have faith, especially the old ones. One man received the 37 practices of the Bodhisattva from Tsara Dharmakirti 15 times. Now he leads hundreds in that practice & *nyungne*. "I'm not good enough" is a common doubt. But one yogi just cleaned the shrine room (& did mantra). When he died there were signs of great realization: his body shrank & there were rainbows. TD taught him some; he was ugly & dirty. Rinpoche teases us: I can talk & you can't!

We are truly in Dewachen, a pristine wilderness of such beauty. Time to drink & eat. Josh moving out; a little talk & a hug.

9:30. Rinpoche gone on a photo shoot for his new book. We meditate without him & then we servers leave early to prep. Ananda was raised by premies, devotees of an Indian guru. She is a nurse; she has MS. Chris raised Catholic in West Palm Beach. Helen didn't sleep. (Tasha is allergic to nuts, has nice toes.)

The carrot & raisin salad is a hit. After lunch, I have a private interview with Rinpoche. Tears come to my eyes: 36 years of practice but no close teacher until now! I confess my doubts the other day & my embarrassment. He says I'm silly, that he felt he could touch me in fun, that I'm so sensitive. He has such beautiful eyes. He says I'm not 9 years old anymore. I say I feel like I am sometimes... I ask about guru yoga again. He says see the big picture, come back & fix parts of the *ngondro* later. He says I need a plan! (I'm not exactly young) OK? Good!

4:45. Kieffer moving into cabin. He's Ananda's husband, a dancer. He can't talk.

5:30. Thunderation! Helen in town with Melissa, closing the purchase of the church on Josephine Street. She showed me the prayer I am supposed to be saying when I do my bows during practice: Visualize the perfect Buddha, adorned on the head, white in color, untouched by fault, whose compassionate eyes watch over beings. I prostrate to Avalokiteshvara. With a thousand arms that have the power of a thousand universal monarchs, & a thousand eyes that have the omniscience of a thousand Buddhas of the excellent kalpa, you guide beings according to their dispositions. I prostrate to the pristine Avalokiteshvara. Om mani padme hung hri...

8:34. Just back from dinner with Rinpoche & the other servers. Helen just got back from closing the deal. Emaho! There was a rainbow!

Tina couldn't talk but looked beautiful, too young for me. She has straight silky blonde hair, nice skin. Overheard her say she wants to move closer to Denver (from Ft. Collins) the other day. Rinpoche says the 6 syllables of the mantra are also the 6 paramitas. He saw bighorns, goats, marmots from Mt. Evans, Denver too, a 360 degree view, with snow. That's where he went, with Greg, a sangha photographer. Helen will very probably not want to spend extra time going up there Saturday.

July 29

Dream of motley crew of cab-drivers with cabs out of *Road Warrior* movie, junky, mismanaged. 5:15, lower back pain, ibuprofen, Kieffer already up. What a good shower & good soap from Sue. It's the last day.

It's dedication of merit day for the end of the *nyungne* & the buying of the church (2 years in the making) & Dharma in the West. Today, every 5 minutes we should dedicate & rejoice. Young Rinpoche had dreams of redheads & blonds. Were they ghosts? No, they were future students in the US. We have a connection from the past he says.

Om mani padme hung hri…

7:26. Going to walk instead of crawling into bag, then do *ngondro*. "There's a bright, golden haze on the meadow." Not really: it's wet, green, elk heaven. Peaks above treeline up above. It's cool in the shade, the sun just coming onto the road. I stop by kitchen & mutely visit Tom, Tina & Leigh Ann who are discussing their menu. Potato-leek soup. "We could be relaxing in my sleeping bag" (the Band). American songs in my head; my culture.

Do little, not even *ngondro*.

Add names to Tasha's prayer list: Rawlins, Cate, Bob.

Rinpoche is by the old rusty vehicle carcass, throwing pebbles into it & into people's shoes. Time for soup. And nuts & the whole vajrayana lunch.

Will is going to do a 3 year retreat in a couple years at Garchen Rinpoche's in Arizona. He spins his prayer wheel. What will await him when he comes out? Extreme times for sure. But also, hopefully: OKL in Denver.

4:25. Considering giving Tina her CD now. I brought 5 with me. 4:50. Shaved, walked, couldn't find Tina but gave one to Ananda. I'm trying to avoid the rush in the morning. I go up to the yurt & silently give Tina *Now Here This* & a card. She's probably thinking what's up with this? 7:08. Saw deer with David S., Chris & Leigh Ann from the yurt deck. No rain yet today. Last night in cabin 3. Thirsty. Do *ngondro*.

July 30

Another anxious dream of cab-driving. I didn't call in after I got my cab & then got side-tracked for a long time. Stole a junker, saw a chess player, heard excellent Clapton Christmas music coming from a church in the barrio. I wake up doubting my sanity at 1 am, do mantra, write. "When encountering disagreeable circumstances, viewing them as illusory is the Bodhisattvas' practice."

3:56. Can't sleep. Was Rinpoche outside my window with a squirtgun? Illusory. Some anxiety; some smiles & laughter too at my situation & thoughts. Is my brain dehydrated? Could drink some water but I want to hold on. Stomach noises. The poor Somalis, their stomachs: Om mani padme hung hri. Am I too old for this? Dedicate the merit.

Patience. Soon I will have raspberry fizzy, tea, soymilk & who knows what all for breakfast.

5:15. Here in yurt early for once; I enter right behind Rinpoche. Soft thunder in stomach. He says we did a wonderful job, that the energy of the practice & the land has changed. He was up reading until 1:30. (he has read 3 books during *nyungne*) His dream: he was walking with a yak in the dark, up a mountain. Then he saw there was a whole country under water & was afraid. A lot of people were being rescued but he thought he couldn't help because he can't swim. He used his hands & flew down & saved some from drowning. Then they wanted money & stabbed him with knives in the 4 directions of his body. He remembered he was keeping *nyungne* vows not to kill. He called on Tsara Dharmakirti. He realized he was dreaming...Wow.

We do 2 long prayers we hadn't done before. I look on with Nancy. We're done!

Breakfast in the cabin & then more in the lodge with the others. Tina doing dishes; we hug & I say I'll email her. Give out CDs to Keiffer, Leigh Ann & Tasha. Pack & clean. Everyone hustling. Melissa back. Go up to yurt where Rinpoche hugs my head & tells me not to be neurotic. "I'll see you in Crestone," he says. I carry his suitcase & long prayer wheel to his vehicle. Helen can't find her cellphone. While she's searching, I learn from Jenka that the bark beetles are getting closer to her wonderful forest. Then Helen drives & we're off on our long trip back to Albuquerque. Put on Bach's Goldberg Variations as I try to rest; glory of the European tradition & genius. Music for piano & Kia.

On the road, Helen says Rinpoche is sensitive, may not approve of his part in this book. I'll have to email him. I say that his dream would make a good ending to the book. She says Tina too young for me. Maybe I could date her friend Debbie in ABQ.

Back home, turn on the swamp cooler, find on Facebook that Tim DeChristopher was sentenced to 2 years, $10,000 fine. "With lives on the line, this is what love looks like, & it will only continue to grow." Thank you, Tim & thank you, thank you Rinpoche.

Chapter 11
Union

July 31, Sunday

Weird dream.

NYT: 25 glaciers left in Glacier National Park. There were 150; all could be gone in 9 years. Impermanent emptiness.

I miss the Buddha, Dharma & Sangha.

Sue: Tom survived his surgery, is doing well. Yesterday, Sue went to beach with 2 moms & 4 kids. She's going to NY Friday for 9 days, will meet Rick at Lake George.

Samsara emails. I open the letter from the clinic. It's my blood test results. WBC = 3.5 out of 4-11; RBC 4.49 out of 4.5-6. No note. As usual, my doctor thinks I'm OK. Take a nap, go to the store. Samsara news. I'm disappointed that nothing has changed. Watch *The Big Lebowski*. A couple laughs.

August 1

Dream of tiger; also I was changing the word BAKED to NAKED (as in Naked Juice). I wake at 4:30 & lie there with my "The Tyger" running through my synapses. Listen to NPR: compromise with fascists possible. Up at 5:30.

Times, "The President Surrenders" by Paul Krugman. "A catastrophe on multiple levels."

Walk to Carlisle & find a pheasant pheather! Where did that come from? Make appointment with Maxx for a haircut. To Nancy: question reality! Call boss. He asks if I finished my book. I say no, I need another 2 months off, should be ready by Balloon Fiesta. He says OK. That was so easy! All those dreams about it…Emaho!

Google myself! I'm there, with songs! Plus Twitter history over 2 years; it's not my thing. Now TH: both sides of the deal, politics, economy. Obama negotiated with crazy hostage takers. George Washington didn't compromise with George III; FDR didn't with Hitler.

Ecobuddhism.org. Bodhgaya, India: October 26–29, 2011. "The Future of Buddhism, From Personal Awakening to Global Transformation." "Many are confronting our rapidly globalizing & interconnecting world by retreating into parochial nationalisms, ideologies of ethnic superiority & religious fundamentalism. Many Buddhists have been part of political campaigns that have killed thousands & forced millions into domestic & international exile. Yet at the same time, an unprecedented number of people in the world are crossing national, ethnic & religious barriers through internet & other technologies to interact, learn & rejoice at our diversity."

China's Cognitive Dissonance on Climate: "Its emissions have more than doubled since 2000."

The Dalai Lama: Focus Should Now Be on Climate Change, not Politics, in Tibet.

A video from Obama for America 2012. He says this chapter is over (but Congress still has to vote on the deal). Randi thinks Obama did well & that down the road taxes will go up on the rich. But CP says: "We not only have no policy to prevent catastrophic climate change, our 'leaders' have stopped talking about the problem & the House is trying to stop anyone from even planning for it." Romm thinks the deal is a disaster.

So many things that OR said are coming back to me. Like focus on yourself first.

12% of US in exceptional drought conditions. Bernie Sanders says 14th amendment should be invoked by the president. 142 killed in Syria over the weekend. Interview by Amy Goodman of Billy Bragg, UK songwriter & activist.

NPR: deal passes House, with Gabby Giffords on the floor. It's expected to pass the Senate too. (will Sanders filibuster I wonder?) 86 degrees. Joe Diaz says the monsoons have failed to develop so far & probably won't. I go on Facebook, looking at friends of friends. Find Tina among others. So many people!

August 2

Tina emails: OMG! She loved the CD, signs off "with much affection," looking forward to the phowa retreat in September. WOW! Tina, Tina, Tina, Tina! My heart & lips sing…

On walk I get dizzy bending over to look at a dead bird. It's a robin; I sit on the curb. On the way back, I kick a little apple down the street & finally into the sewer. I pick a sunflower from Gabby's profusion of sunflowers. "Dizzy Miss Lizzy": "tell your mama I want you to be my bride…give me fever, you look so fine…I wish you were mine." John Lennon singing.

I write her, sign it "love." Write Helen too. Tibetan women singing.

Go to Wild Birds Unlimited & buy 20 pounds of seed for $18.

Debt deal passes Senate & Obama signs it. It could be 110 in Dallas today. Lie down after lunch, fixated on Tina…

But after haircut I wanted to kiss Maxx! I told her she got her beauty from her mom. She said to keep in touch, we could have coffee sometime. She just started antibiotics for bronchitis, had a nice book from the Kalachakra empowerment in DC.

Shannon calls! Her sister's wedding is at the end of September, in Cancun! Shannon needs to get a passport. She says she has a hard time with Buddhism because of the way she was brought up! But she appreciates that she was exposed to it too. She saw *Unmistaken Child* & loved it.

Mostly Mozart on PBS. Helen approves of my email to Rinpoche.

August 3

Wake at 5. Thoughts of women & my physical weakness during preliminary practices.

"Too Many People" by Paul McCartney. Wild humans unlimited? How many kids does he have? I walk to I-40 bridge for elevation past the lonely larch tree. Four hot air balloons float in the distance. I'm not that weak; maybe it's just low blood pressure.

Write. Remember Doolittle Ranch.

I watch Post Carbon Institute video on the end of economic growth by Richard Heinberg & suddenly get very tired. We have overshot the limits to growth. Samsara to the nth. Suffering & death. Om mani padme hung hri.

Send postcard to Tim in prison.

Bernie calls. He'll come to Chokor duchen tonight at Scott's he says; his friend was staying at a motel. He asks about *nyungne* & tells me about Anam Thubten coming this weekend.

Rain getting close, it cools down to 70.

149

ABC News: Killer heat, 100 dead, ERs overrun, 114 in Ft. Smith, 2 high school football players died. Mubarak faces death penalty, in a stretcher in a cage in Cairo courtroom. 36 million pounds of ground turkey recalled for salmonella. Mormons say Garden of Eden was in Missouri (2 of them running for president). The other side: near-death experiences. Local: Jemez Springs getting flooded.

The party. I call Cate & we drive together. She says she's not depressed just crazy with despair, never relaxes. Nice woman, Sally, is at the duchen. David explains that his book might get published by Shamballa but turns away in the middle of my description of my book! I'm flabbergasted! He's a trip. Finally, the rain lets up so Carol & Corey lead the smoke offering & worm release. Gary doesn't join in; he's into Dzogchen only…Bernie doesn't show up. Home at 9:45.

August 4

Sleep till 7, then nap from 9:30 to 11:30. Groggy, I read email from Tina signed "love." She's in Georgia, visiting her mother. She graduated from Naropa but just got a M.Div. degree from somewhere.

2,000 a day are dying in Somalia. Avaaz.org updates signers of its petition to end the famine as I watch. About one per second for a while, mostly from EU & North America. I share on Facebook: stop the famine!

To Tina: tell me more about M.Div., how is your mother?, Extreme Times = the degenerate age. Tina/Maxx? "Not to engage in subject-object duality is the Bodhisattvas' practice."

Rick calls. The lake is warmer than last year. They have been there 2 weeks; 2 weeks to go. Second cousin, John Thompson, plays in 3 bands, works at solar power monitoring over the internet. Elevation at Lake George is 300 ft.

5:30. Om mani padme hung hri. Market meltdown. Down 512 with fears of a new recession. Also, record heat is stressing people & the grid. Syria. Astronomy: new theory says there were two moons once. Local: normal precipitation, 4.94 for year; so far, .70. Average high for this time of year is 88; it's going to 96 soon. China cyberattacks.

Call Maxx. She's got a cough. Her duchen stupa consecration in Truth or Consequences was good. I'll call Saturday for maybe coffee.

August 5

Mixed up dreams: caves, prehistoric rituals.

Infinite beings & I are alike in so many ways & yet I am unique…

I see a merlin (or something) on a rooftop. He flies right at me!

NYT: Shell Gets Tentative Approval to Drill in Arctic.

Bernie Sanders on TH, a moral voice in the congressional wilderness. He voted against the debt deal, fears the cuts.

Thoughts turn to Tina, genetrix from Georgia. It's raining a bit. I want to snuggle. 48 days till I see her & OR in Crestone. "Dharma is the best girlfriend."

Shannon calls. She had the wrong number copied for my new credit/debit card. She mentions Joanna Macy (as did Tina). I find my book, bought in 2001 on last visit to San Francisco.

I start reading *World as Lover, World as Self*, then sit. Maybe I shouldn't lie down anymore but practice. I'd like to do 30,000 mantras next week.

Craig calls & talks me into a chess tournament in Santa Fe in 2 weeks.

CP: NOAA: Prepare for "High Hurricane Activity" in the Atlantic; Bombshell: Warming May Shrink Russian Permafrost 30% by 2050; SpongeBob Squarepants, Cartoon Invertebrate, is Smarter Than Murdoch's Fox News Hominids.

August 6, Hiroshima Day

I was sick & needed a certain kind of tea. Dream.

Call Maxx: she just bought a Mac, coffee another time.

A message from APR to read *Words of My Perfect Teacher* & be mindful. I practice extra then go to Hastings & rent *Uncle Boonmee Who Can Recall His Past Lives*. To Whole Foods. Marie checks me out & I eat there in an unreal newspaper/desire fog.

Home to an anxious nap.

30 US dead as helicopter shot down in Afghanistan. Standard & Poor's downgrades US credit rating to AA+.

Uncle Boonmee is an ultra-slow movie, with no music & little Thai dialogue. Lots of crickets, but I don't see that Uncle Boonmee recalled even one past life…

August 7

Photos on Facebook of 3300 Josephine St., OR & sangha.

NYT: "The hardest part is that just to stay in the game, I have to scrutinize my every thought, every attitude, every emotion, everything, & ask 'Is this real?'" —Joe Holt, 50, on his struggles with schizophrenia.

Degrees of insanity.

I've changed the name of the old Joan Baez song "Dona Dona" to "Dena Dena" & now to "Tina Tina" (I love you). Longing for love, passive & active. Om namah kali ma. Love the guru. Om tare tam soha with Copper Mountain four. All I need is love. I wonder if I even have a book.

Then to Helen & Michael's (they saw *Uncle Boonmee* too) Melinda comes & we listen to audio from OR, secret teachings on Buddha Nature, & discuss.

After, I take a side trip to Piedra Lisa Trailhead, wearing sandals & one of Michael's cowboy hats. It's too hot to walk anyway. Great holy mountain. Silence of blazing sun. Without oil I couldn't be here. Desert island, some moisture up past these granite cliffs. But down here: the naked truth of the ground.

Home to message from Rawlins: he's moving to Silver City! Email from Tina: she says her family is pretty insane. She's an interfaith chaplain!

5:30, 95 degrees. Men lost in Afghanistan: elite, tears, widows, the word "enemy." What are we doing in their country again? Governments brace; investors shouldn't panic. Verizon strike; London burning; Africa; Boeing 787. Another newscast with not even a mention of what we have to do for a future, let alone any urgency.

CP on Drew Westen's *NYTimes* piece: we needed an FDR & we got a compromiser.

Really hot tonight. I'm drawn to Denver by two longings, for temporary & ultimate happiness. AH.

August 8

Sleep through alarm; tea at 7.

"Even hearers & solitary realizers, who accomplish only their own welfare, strive as if putting out a fire on their heads. Seeing this, taking up diligent effort—the source of good qualities—for the sake of all beings is the Bodhisattvas' practice."

Send Tina an email but I feel sad I can't express love & that the world is so full of suffering. As OR says, "it's the 21st century." I practice but feel neurotic during it. Oh well, me & infinite beings. Two hour anxious nap.

World markets plunge; Dow down 635. Krugman on PBS; riots in UK.

August 9

Wake at 4:37. I think I'm not dreaming so much since I ran out of B vitamins. Get some today.

9:44, arrive at source of Travertine Falls, 44 minutes after leaving a message from Tina. Cougar country; bear country. Walk loudly & carry a big stick. Even in the superdrought the mountain has water! Where the heck does it come from? A hummer, a jay, a magic spot to set up my sitting pad. Shady trees, a squirrel. If only my old knees would cooperate. Jane, at Copper Mountain, was talking about a class with a student of Tom Brown, the tracker. Big wings above in the tree. Sit silently with death, an inaudible mountain lion, behind me. This could be my last breath, for you, lion, robins coming to drink. AH. The grapevine of faith clings to the great & glorious juniper of the lama! Emaho!

CP: After Praying for Rain, Texas Governor Rick Perry Prays for the EPA to Stop Environmental Regulations; 90 Degree River Shuts Down Tennessee Nuclear Plant for Second Time; EIA: High temperatures drove record electricity demand & very high wholesale prices in Texas...

And now back to the financial collapse... Truly, we have overshot the limits to growth (the cause) & we will have to bear the consequences (the effect). Mass ignorance causes mass suffering.

Wrote Tina, saying call. It's been 8 days since she wrote first (OMG!).

Am I so tired because of meds? RBC? Old age? Who knows? Tell me. Imagine love from Guru Rinpoche, APR, OR…

Sue calls! It's a cloudy day at Lake George. Rick saw barred owls, heard the hermit thrush… They wish I could be there & I do too, but I'm trying to keep my carbon footprint small…

Hottest temperature the past week was 122 in Saudi Arabia. Typhoon Muifa hit China. Wolves return to France after 80 years of eradication. Tropical Storm Don Fizzles on Texas Coast: "the extremely arid condition left by months of parching drought caused the storm to virtually evaporate when it made landfall…"

Earthtreasurevase.org. Inspired by an ancient Tibetan Buddhist tradition, the Earth Treasure Vase Global Healing Project brings healing & protection to the Earth by filling consecrated clay vessels with prayers & offerings, & ceremonially burying them… Cynthia Jurs is the director; she started with 30 vases & now 23 are buried around the planet…

96 degrees, 6% humidity here.

London burning—invest like a girl. Oklahoma average for July was 89.1 degrees, highest for any state. Stocks up 430. Fuel efficiency going up thanks to Obama. 500 arrests in UK; 16,000 officers. Flashmobs. Syrian dissident: we use cameras, they use guns. 200,000 girls have signed up for girlup.com—girl-to-girl across the world.

August 10

Riding a bicycle, couldn't decide to turn left or right, ran into another bike, a woman. Perfection of universe, not one quark left out. I had B vitamins with dinner.

"The Inuit have a word for the weather now: *uqqianaqtuq*. This means 'not its usual self.'"

TH depressed: only 2 Wisconsin Republican state senators were recalled out of 6. $40m spent by oligarch on misleading TV ads. No matter what happens in the future, what's happening right now is the perfection of the universe. But the media is depressing…

I play a little, practicing for tomorrow with Nick. Lie down but anxious. Practice getting used to mind. Now time to go to moveon.org protest downtown.

A bunch of old people (me included). The Raging Grannies sing a couple of their songs but it's not music to my ears. Eric Griego & Jerry

Ortiz y Pino speak briefly. 100 people? Ten steps to get the economy back on track: 1. invest in America's infrastructure 2. create 21st century energy jobs 3. invest in public education 4. offer Medicare for all 5. make work pay 6. secure social security 7. return to fairer tax rates 8. end the wars & invest at home 9. tax Wall St. speculation 10. strengthen democracy.

Home in time for the *NewsHour*. Dow down 500.

Rawlins calls. He's going to live with Michael Brown who is into alternative healing & native healers for his leukemia

August 11

Dream of pi multiples (3.14). 15.70, the age of Vajrayogini. Also nice Sunnie (Shannon's mom) & a book about the Grand Canyon. 1884: Joyce was 2. 2198: where will I be? Magical pi. Maybe I should get a piece of pie at Flying Star.

Print "Her Eyes Were Like Crystal" (1974) (for Sandra a.k.a. Mary). Off to get Nick.

We record "Her Eyes," "Mirror," "Angels" & "The Force" (Dylan Thomas lyric). Positive feedback from Nick. Maybe I should do a house concert. At Helen's?

Nothing from Tina. She's probably getting up the courage to call.

> *Unless the sun of devotion shines*
> *On the snow peak of the teacher's four kayas,*
> *The stream of his blessings will never flow.*
> *So earnestly arouse devotion in your mind!*

> —Drikung Kyobpa Rinpoche

I started thinking about going to DC, 9 days away from now. Lora is going she says; Mark Ruffalo is too (video on Facebook). I could stay at brother Jon's, 100 miles away... Crazy idea, save the gas. I'm too old & tired. But I hope the Bos-Wash people get into it big time.

New OR website! Sweet! Buddha, Dharma & Sangha, a big sangha, with kids.

Super Committee all appointed now (only one woman, of 12). Compromise possible says Andrea Seabrook. Cameron speaks to parliament, resists investigation; Milliband agrees. Wow: 100 degrees at UNM. Is there dinner? Yes, fungus & chocolate.

Child labor on US farms. Price of cottage cheese spurs Israeli protests from Tel Aviv to other cities. Iceberg tourism & iceberg beer in Newfoundland. Short selling banned in 4 EU nations. Then on PBS: *Grand Canyon Serenade*—time lapse chopper views accompanied by Satie & Dvorak instead of chopper noise. I took several backpacking trips there in the 70s. Never did the river run though, like these people. No man's geology-land. Been there! Back when nobody knew about global warming & we could imagine a future if we could just get rid of nukes. $60 contribution gets you a DVD.

August 12

Dreams. End of a *nyungne*, starving kids in Santa Fe, feed them. Playing happy birthday on a small, stupid keyboard. Telling a little kid about brushing & flossing. Asking young girl if I could have some of her non-existent breast milk. Wow, those B vitamins.

Tina is not a phone person she says. Disappointing. She's brief but still signs "love."

NYT: copper thieves are stealing AC coils from churches, etc. "When you're bleeding profusely from an open wound, you want a doctor who binds that wound up, not a doctor who lectures you on the importance of maintaining a healthy lifestyle as you get older." —Paul Krugman

Many thoughts of many women. Dedicate my little merit & get up. Ready a CD for Eliza Gilkyson, care of Red House Records. Maybe she'll listen.

Idea: drop book, too personal. Too lonely.

August 13

Dream of George, my old bass player friend. Losing a boy from cab.

Drop this book? Let me think about it. Eviscerated dove by the wisteria. The merlin (formerly known as the pigeon hawk) probably got it. Compassion for the falcon, driven by genes, long evolution. It has to eat.

Beautiful photos of OKL in Denver. Rinpoche & Melissa look like a painting on the wall as they sit in the shrine alcove. One picture of OR as Guru Rinpoche, wide-eyed & wrathful.

Write T. & Shan. Tell Tina I'm going to sing & I do. Resurrect some old songs, "Free Tibet," "Everything Is Perfect," "Love Your Love"…

To library for 3 good DVDs. Mail Eliza a CD & then get one, from Marie! I'm in love again, anxiety in stomach blown away by the vision of the young lady & her sweetness. The CD is *Oil & Glitter* by the band she's in, Shoulder Voices. Home to rain; I turn off the cooler to hear it better.

Dharmakaya = emptiness
Samboghakaya = awareness
Nirmanakaya = thoughts

I watch *The Iceberg*, French fable with slapstick. Good laughs.

Still raining at news time. Chris calls! He was gone for 2 weeks, to Paris & England. He walked 5 miles on his bad knee in the Cotswold Hills. He might want to see Kalu Rinpoche when he comes in September.

Finish 30,500 mantras for the week.

August 14

Dream of a big guitar class. G minor improvisations by students, some of which are incredible. Big auditorium; Howard Schultz sits by me.

"*Ngondro* is the storyline that prepares us to get the punch line—in this case, the pointing-out instructions that introduce us to the actual practice of the nature or the mind." —Dzogchen Ponlop Rinpoche.

I send the quote to Tina, signed "love you."

Man, I'm going to cry. Printing up old songs about Mom, Shanny. I do cry, for pain gone by & missing my daughter & remembering that OR told her I was a good dad.

Drive to Helen & Michael's listening to Marie's meaningless CD. I know I'm causing suffering through CO_2, climate change. Vajrasattva mantra for myself & others, trapped in this age.

Chaotic session with Michael jumping around the audio file & Melinda asking questions (she's in pain from back) & me feeling guilty for global warming & sleepy.

* * *

157

Beethoven in *Eroica* DVD: hot-headed, romantic genius (20 years before the 9th). No one clapped at the end of the rehearsal. He said thank you & went back to work. And I'm back to being alone again. Take a sunset walk…

August 15

Dream of eating a giant grape. Stupa area, shortage of food & water. (CP: US corn, wheat & soy harvests down 5% due to climate)

Tina writes that she feels "forlorn." And "love you." Oh baby, let's get together & be forlorn together.

Warren Buffett writes "Stop Coddling the Super-Rich" in NYT. FB, Guardian: 1,500 have signed on to risk arrest over tar sands, coming this Saturday.

Write Tina, signed "Yours in the dharma, love you."

Words from crossword: elate, beanpole, ease, frozen tundra, lean on me, octopi, hi hat, wed, Sade, groan, backrub, basil, chaos, tide, tomb, zoom. I'm an elated beanpole over Tina, as the frozen tundra melts… Want to wed?

Could I go to see OR on September 10? (& see Tina?) How much money?

Thinkprogress.org/romm. Cryosphere changes as Shell prepares to drill in Arctic. China will double its solar capacity to around 2 GW by the end of the year. Pollution or no pollution, oil production goes on in Ogoni (Nigeria). Obama administration to launch Brazil energy partnership (oil & gas). Presidential candidate Gov. Rick Perry (R-TX): global warming is "all one contrived phony mess."

Randi on the obscene wealth inequality in the US & the obscene Republicans.

Print up some more old songs. Marie, are you in this band because you like Bobby's music or just to have a gig? I hope you're not a victim of meaninglessness…

ABC-TV: Weather Gone Wild. Arctic ice smallest ever in July; 10 inches of rain in Long Island; heat records; snow in New Zealand. But nothing on fossil fuels, hmm. Big violent gust in Indiana kills 5 at a concert. PBS: lots of death in Iraq & Afghanistan. Shell oil spill in North Sea. Rebel advances in Libya.

I call Sue; she's back in Florida.

I take no trazadone.

First part of the night: endless thoughts, then the refuge prayer dream understanding...

August 16

Cab dream too. Hard to get up.

Have I said too much to Tina? (wanting a girlfriend) No! She replies with love. She finished her *ngondro* in 4 years, is doing guru yoga now.

6.854 billion humans. China, 1.3 billion; India, 1.2 billion; US, .3 billion.

2,000+ commitments for civil disobedience at the White House now. Lora will be there.

Two more old songs. Memories. Joey would be 32 or so now.

Can't watch all the news...

No traz but can't get to sleep. Craig calls at 9:30. I take 50 mg. & sleep.

August 17

Flood; also a dog the size of a mouse, named Gary. Up early (5:40).

Nothing from Tina. Sadness. It's cloudy. Thinking of going to the Albuquerque stupa; it wouldn't be too hot.

Food & Water Watch: "Are there 'nanopesticides' in your food?" R. forwards me Avaaz.org petition to save the Amazon.

CP: S&P Downgrades Planet Earth & Humanity, Citing Unbalanced Carbon Budget, Reckless Political Debates & Role of "Deniers" (by Chris Mooney). From HHH, the only one in the galaxy, to HH+ (H is for habitable). Then Joe Romm: "in related move, S&P downgraded humanity from the subspecies nomenclature *Homo sapiens sapiens* to *Homo sapiens*...we are also recommending putting the other one in quotes, so we are *Homo 'sapiens,'* at least until we see whether we are in fact smart enough to save ourselves from self-destruction."

87.4 million barrels/day, peak (so far) of oil consumption in 2010. And now this reporter will use some more: to the petroglyphs!

The stupa is a 10 foot high, white monument representing the Enlightened Mind. It's off in the ragged desert near the Petroglyph National Monument Visitors Center. There used to be a house & a trailer beside it before the National Monument was established. The National Park Service said the stupa could remain. There's a controversy now about First Amendment rights etc. It's simple & sweet, pennies line the tiers of the stupa as offerings & there is a small statue of Buddha & a photo in the alcove near the mid-section. I half-expect a rattlesnake to strike my unprotected toes. I'm at the base of volcanic cliffs with 24,000 rock drawings; some could be as old as 3000 years.

Patrick Vigil, the ranger in the Visitors Center, is a Zen Buddhist! He says you can see moss growing in some of the volcanoes where mist comes up. He drives to the Zen Center twice a day.

Ideas for a banner to hold in front of Channel 7: 1. FOSSIL FUEL = CLIMATE CHANGE, 2. JOE DIAZ: QUIT SMILING & TALK ABOUT CLIMATE CHANGE, 3. JOE DIAZ —YOU CAN COUNT ON CLIMATE CHANGE, 4. GET RID OF E.T. & AIR HALF HOUR OF CLIMATE SCIENCE EACH NIGHT, 5. TV: COVER THE DC CLIMATE PROTEST, 6. CORPORATE MEDIA HIDES CLIMATE CHANGE.

Savetibet.org. "In a second reported self-immolation this year, Tsewang Norbu, a 29 year old Tibetan monk from Nyitso monastery…died on Aug. 15 after setting himself on fire to protest Chinese rule in Tibet."

BBC: Anna Hazare, anti-corruption campaigner in India, is in prison, fasting. Huge protests in the streets. PBS: Wealth inequality in US caused crash of '08 & it still exists.

Nice rain.

August 18

Dream of snowy mountains.

Jason Box, climate scientist, will join the DC protests. Akilah says to call her re protest here.

I go back to bed after walk & fall asleep. Dream of Santa Fe stupa, that I have to pay a charge for Dawa, my old dog, & a car parked there. I owe overdue bills for that! Now it's almost noon.

Print up "Song of the Hopi" & others. What a prophecy!

I cling to women today: R., T., Sally, Akilah! So what else is new? Emptiness clinging to emptiness…

New *Sierra* magazine in the mailbox. "Everything is flowing — going somewhere, animals & so-called lifeless rocks as well as water." — John Muir

Call Sue. She's getting an MRI for her brain to check on ringing in her ears.

August 19

Dream of a dark-haired woman who wants my baby & I'm in love with her. 3:43, forgot the rest.

Tina writes! Signs it "good night XO."

NYT. "Longer Lives for Obese Mice, with Hope for Humans of All Sizes." Resveratrol mimics.

Imagine a future in another body, on another planet maybe. "Everything possible to be believed is an image of the truth." —William Blake. Hitler is God? Well, both are patriarchal, heirarchal concepts. Black is white? No black without white…

Bernie Sanders on TH: Bodhisattva speaks. Solar, clean energy, jobs not Tar Sands.

To Whole Foods for Adrenal Support pills, wave at Marie. McKibben with Nicole Sandler (in for Randi): he teaches Sunday school & believes in prayer as long as you are not doing things that make the prayer harder to answer, like Gov. Perry does. He will be arrested tomorrow.

The slow parts of the Magnificat make me think I'm dying. Yawn, bleary-eyed, & lie down. But get up for "Wachet auf (wake up)." Wedding of Soul & Jesus; so sweet. "Let love bring no division." Non-duality there but eternalism is a problem. Maybe Bach became a Zen monk his next lifetime. 1685-1750.

News: Bill Clinton is a VEGAN! Another giant duststorm in Phoenix. Glen Campbell has Alzheimer's.

Call Ariel & arrange to visit after Copper Mountain on Sunday.

August 20

Drive to Santa Fe for chess tournament that Craig is going to. Win the first game on time; lose second to Carlos who is rated 2022. Win third over Gene, who didn't see my mate threat. Lose next one to Dante (1878); his combination got my queen. Twelve year old Harsh (happiness) from India upsets Carlos. The time given to you on your clock is based on the difference between ratings. I was given a rating of 1622 for the tournament since I haven't played a rated game in so long.

I wonder how it's going in DC. Obama on vacation but Bill McKibben has probably been booked & released for trespassing or whatever the agreement with the police is.

I beat Bill on time but played well. Next, Craig, Mr. Nervous. I wish that all beings could relax (including me). Om tare tutare ture soha. Be free of fear, all beings! Check! In the room it's whispers, laughter, sighs. A-h, 1-8: a dance of polarities. I might lose on time; I only have 5 minutes to Craig's 55. But he's mated, after ignoring a building threat when he could have defended. One must relax to see the truth.

Off to Chris & Christine's. Teen is drinking a margarita after canning. We eat a "Gerald" pizza with zucchini & other garden vegetables. Yum. Talk of chess, Christine's daughter in Ghana, my uncertain future.

Flashes & thunder in the mid-night.

August 21

First news on the protest is from Lora via FB: lots of photos but not much else. Then a Nation story: 70 busted. "If all the oil were extracted overnight it would increase the carbon in the earth's atmosphere from 393 ppm to 550 ppm —a devastating increase." Arrested include Bill, Jane Hamsher (FireDogLake), Lt. Dan Choi, Gus Speth. "Hey hey, ho ho, Keystone XL's got to go."

Tina got the job at Naropa!

Copper Mountain. Scott acts as chopen for Green Tara practice. Then to see Ariel, Ruby & 4 year old Flannery. Cancer survivors. Girls. Ruby wants to come to Copper Mountain; Ariel wants to get into eco-stuff again. (We met at the Interfaith Power & Light booth once, both volunteers.) Ruby more attractive, sweet mom.

Phowa practice at 4. Just three of us.

Lora arrested. She paid $100 fine.

162

August 22

Dream of a fungus that is aware! Everybody loves it...

NYT editorial opposes pipeline but doesn't mention protest—Jubilant Rebels Control Much of Tripoli.

FB link to NYT, Aug. 19: "Protest Makes Canada-to-US Pipeline Project Newest Front in Climate Clash."

TH: protest leads; Thom thinks Obama will approve pipeline.

I call Craig. I tell him I'll be his chess coach for a fee. It will involve relaxation. He's open to it. Also tell him about October 21 OR Green Tara empowerment. Who knows? Maybe he will start meditating & relax...

1 pm, CNN radio: MLK Monument in DC is open now.

5, NPR: Ghaddafi's whereabouts unknown; there is still fighting in Tripoli; Ghaddafi was 42 years in power; Hurricane Irene coming to SE US; PBS: AmericansElect.org, an online nominating process for president.

August 23

Dream of transcendent music; get up with Bach in my head. Pick up guitar & get a new song! The moon is high / A bright white eye / Down here below / I miss you so / The sun comes up / Red eye of love / It shines on earth / Today's rebirth / It's all in blue / blue eye of truth / I'm one with you / The dream comes true (in pure view) (do, few, jewel, new) It's not exactly Bach but it'll do...Title? "Third Eye"? "Union"?

See 2 angels on walk: Gabrielle & doggie.

Energynow.com. Daryl Hannah, actress & environmental advocate, is heading to White House Oil-Sands Protest. As of Monday night, 162 people arrested.

Amy is a geophysicist at USGS! And a sangha member of OR. Earthquakes in Trinidad CO & Washington DC (TH's studio). Caused by fracking? 5.9 magnitude. Felt as far away as Toronto. Rebels in Ghaddafi's compound. The multi-fronted war between love & hate, reason & ignorance goes on. Republicans will push for tax hike on working people.

CP: Absurd *NYTimes* Story on Green Jobs Ignores "Explosive Growth" Documented in the Sector. Vietnam's rice bowl threatened by rising seas.

Tarsandsaction.org: Canadian actors Margot Kidder & Tantoo Cardinal among 60 arrested.

I buy quercetin to see if it will help with tiredness.

Mind's eye is blue / I'm one with you / So clear I see / You're one with me

98 degrees at the Sunport. Ghaddafi still at large. Niece Libby on Bahamas cruise in path of Hurricane Irene. PBS: medical pot. Epilepsy patient loves it. THC receptors all through the body; the body makes cannabinoids in small quantities. May be good for MS, cancer.

No traz.

August 24

Awake at 4:30 with dreams of the Leibman brothers, old musical friends from Boston. Sleep till 7.

Play the new song, adding mantra Om ah hung vajra guru padme siddhi hung. Go to woods.

"We have to wake up to the desperate & miserable conditions of this age; instead of finding it a source of fascination & pleasure, we ought to feel like a fish writhing on a hook. We need to turn to Guru Rinpoche, the perfect buddha who vowed especially to help beings of these decadent times, & call out to him with ardor & with longing: 'There is no other hope for me but you! Unless you take me under your protection, I shall sink even deeper into samsara's ocean of suffering.' This is how the sun of Guru Rinpoche's compassion, concentrated through the magnifying glass of our devotion, will set fire to the dry grass of our ignorance & destructive emotions." —Dilgo Khyentse Rinpoche, *Guru Yoga*.

Next time I'm bringing a sandwich. Who wants to leave this peaceful ponderosa community? The ants, the flies, the chickadees, the atmosphere…but Shannon said she'd call this afternoon & I didn't bring phone. I hope she doesn't want money.

Home to start second draft of this book. I'd rather be meditating.

No call from the unpredictable, lovable daughter. But a card, a check & photos from dependable Sue. Only $43k left in that account…That's 43 months at a thousand per month. Anxiety creeps in; I've got to work.

Irene targets Bahamas; 65 million people should get ready. Snipers in Tripoli; hunger in the US: one in four US kids don't have enough food. The recession caused the number of people on food stamps to shoot from 26 million to 46 million.

Nothing from Craig so I drive to the Frontier Restaurant for the chess club alone. Play Ben & Gabe: 2 wins.

Lie down at 9 but get up at 10 & take traz.

Wake at 4 with cell phone beeping because of low battery. Listen to KUNM free-form music. Get up at 5:30. Jupiter straight up. *Ngondro* & creativity (song). I'm in a delicate balance between sleep & waking, calm & activity. Nap from 8:30 to 10.

Koch Brothers own scattered chemical facilities, high risk. E.g. chlorine bleach at paper companies. They are a security risk too. 20,000 people died at Bhopal. The Kochs lobby for less regulations. Greenpeace.org.

CP: conditions for the first 52 arrestees against the tar sands. "Said Mary Nicol of Chicago, who with 14 other women went 17 hours without food at one point & slept in the concrete cell with no bed at all or chairs or sheets: 'It was really rough, but not nearly as rough as life will be for all people everywhere on the planet if Obama doesn't stop this pipeline & halt radical climate change.'"

Center for Biological Diversity: "the world is closing in on a spooky milestone projected for Halloween: 7 billion people."

Shanny calls! They are going to drive to Seattle to house sit for Aaron's cousin! They will be down here tomorrow.

August 26

Red light of love.

"It's hard to see any end to the ongoing economic disaster." — Krugman.

"One must not only preach a sermon with his voice. He must preach it with his life." —MLK.

CP: 275 total arrests at White House.

Shostakovitch Symphony #5. I write; the days run into each other in my "Die or E" but I guess that's how words are, always rushing forward. Even if I put space   between   them. How can I describe the space? Stop your eyes on this upcoming dot & rest there for 5 seconds.

5:30, waiting for kids. ABCTV: 65 million people bracing for a historic storm. Evacuations in Bos-Wash. NYCity could get 15 foot surge with the new moon high tide. The ground is saturated in the Northeast from 12 inches of rain already (normal is 4 inches). BBC: Japanese politics is also "broken." Obama cuts short his vacation on Martha's Vineyard.

With the kids to Orchid Thai then back to unload van. Stuff being stored here include 2 bags of Beanie Babies! Then they have to drive back to Taos. I held my daughter's hand for a whole 5 minutes in the car. She said it reminded her of grandma. They'll be back Monday on their way to Santa Barbara for a wedding.

August 27, Saturday

Pipeline finally makes front page of the *NYTimes* with photo of protesters. "All signs point to the Obama administration approving the project by the end of the year..." The article is mostly favorable toward the pipeline (10,000 jobs). Report says no significant environmental impact! Is global warming too subtle for them?

Tina slept outside last night; wrote at 6:20 this morning. She said I could spearhead the Buddhist rock genre.

Go to Solar Fiesta at Albuquerque Academy, prep school. It's a beautiful campus; Akilah goes here. Meet Tammy at Sierra Club table & sign her petition to Mayor Berry. (Don't roll back the energy efficiency standards for the city) A pamphlet from electricauto.org says world oil production peaked in 97! Lots of electric cars lined up there. Then I meet Ray Powell, NM Commissioner of Public Lands, at the auditorium where he is about to speak. He's a mellow guy with a brown beard.

He asks about the bumpersticker I'm holding: Got Social Security? Thank Democrats (he's a Democrat himself).

He gives a short talk about how his office raises $500 million a year for public schools, hospitals & universities. He was elected again last year after some time working with Jane Goodall's Roots & Shoots environmental education. The last 8 months he has spent mopping up messes from the previous commissioner (Republican). 90% of the revenue is

166

from oil & gas. I ask about fracking & he says they are racing to catch up to the gas companies & make sure it's safe. I want to say: keep fossil fuels in the ground!

The Solar Fiesta is mostly for homeowners with the money to invest in photovoltaics. That leaves me out.

Home to finish my 20,000 vajra guru mantras for this week & study the lineage for tomorrow.

Hurricane worries & fears. But it wasn't so bad in North Carolina. There's a pre-season NFL game on CBS.

Rick calls, back in San Francisco. He & Gloria picked blackberries today & he's making a pie for her birthday tomorrow. He may visit me in October. But after we say goodbye I feel like I'm the sibling rivalry loser, that I couldn't really say what was important to me… AH…

August 28

Dream: dangerously senile Mom transforms into 3 year old Shannon who wants to do it herself. Later in dreams: a female guru who looks straight at us & shows her breasts! It's hard to get up in the dark plus I'm attached to the guru…

Compassion for oneself is a great part of bodhicitta. So one can have compassion for others.

To Copper Mountain. Ariel said that Ruby just had surgery so they couldn't come. I lead the discussion group on the first Dodrubchen, Gyalwe Nyuku, Patrul Rinpoche & Dorje Ziji Tsel. Jane asks how many enlightened people are on earth. At one in a million it would be 7,000. I say I know one in Colorado!

Go by Whole Foods & meet Klassie, beautiful new cashier. She's thinking over what her favorite bird is.

CP: Joe Romm on "why I blog." His ultimate reason is because it's not too late. McKibben: "Jim Hansen gets arrested Monday, Irene willing."

I write a new part to "Union." Will try multi-tracking song with Nick Tuesday.

Message to Lora: do you want to hold a sign at Channel 7 saying "Cover Climate Change"?

5:16, 93 degrees. 86 is the normal. Precipitation at 1.40 out of 6.17 normal.

4.5 million homes & businesses are in the dark on the east coast. Major flooding. A Red Cross ship docks at Tripoli.

Watch a DVD from the library, *The Road to Wellville*. It's hilarious, a satire on the Kellogg Sanitarium in 1880 or so. "An erection is the flagpole on your grave." Nice breasts shown.

August 29

"…The odds are that one of these years the world's greatest nation will find itself ruled by a party that is aggressively anti-science, indeed anti-knowledge. And, in a time of severe challenges—environmental, economic & more —that's a terrifying prospect." —Paul Krugman.

$7 billion damage from Irene; 21 deaths.

Make that 35 deaths.

PBS: tar sands pipeline debate between McKibben & Robert Bryce of the Manhattan Institute. Bill: 500 arrests now to save the climate. Bryce: GHGs will go up anyway so we might as well use the tar sands. It will create jobs. Bill: there is a deeper realism at work here… But Bill seems depressed to have to debate an idiot.

And I'm too depressed to call Sue. Houston sets all-time record of 109 degrees.

I do phowa. Get some perspective.

August 30

Wake up early & McKibben is on the Bill Press show. He's definitely working on it.

Nothing from Tina. Schubert's 9th symphony playing. I'm longing for a smile, a touch. There's a photo of OR holding two kids upside down (Alaya & Ezra) with a smile. I whistle Schubert.

I also wish for a better voice next lifetime, for the benefit of all. I practice singing a bit, then mail my CD to second cousin in Vermont & pick up Nick. We record "Union" but try an extra guitar track which takes too long. He makes $40 for 2 hours work. I'm anxious about money & not understanding the phone bill. I'm anxious about the 21st century, a fish on a hook.

168

260 roads in VT closed plus 30 bridges destroyed. 3.3 million people have no power. Here: 97 degrees today broke record.

I call my sister & watch *Wuthering Heights* till 10. The thin line between love & hate.

August 31

NYT: Exxon Reaches Arctic Oil Deal With Russians.

Atmospheric CO_2 is 392.39 ppm for July 2011.

"We must redefine the meaning of our practice so we can cultivate a feeling of rejoicing about the moment of death." —OR. Wow. And rejoicing about the moments of life.

CP: NASA's James Hansen Arrested at Tar Sands Pipeline Protest.

Am I urgent enough? "Teach us to care & not to care," said T.S. Eliot, i.e. do good things but don't worry about the results. Krishna said something like that too. Buddha said that good actions will have good results, you can count on it.

5, new Japanese news, NHK World. Katherine Kobayashi is the beautiful anchor, in Tokyo.

Chess Club: draw with Chris Cruz.

September 1

Still nada from Tina. I'm going to U Mound for a little hike. Don't see any snakes; play my recorder for a minute while sitting on a rock.

I see an old dharma friend from Santa Fe in Walgreen's where I go to finally buy new sunglasses.

CP: German Renewable Power Production Hits Record High: 20.8%, Quadruple the Level in 2000, on Track to 35% in 2020. Governor Peter Shumlin (D-VT): "We've got to get off fossil fuels as quickly as we know how, to make this planet livable for our children & grandchildren."

Don Henley: "You can't get the genie back in the bottle."

5, Ghaddafi still on the loose. Cesium 137 in Japanese soil with a half-life of 30 years. (I just want to watch Katherine) 100,000 people evacuated. Typhoon approaches Japan. Slow moving Lee may dump 20 inches of rain on New Orleans.

I watch *The Girl with the Pearl Earring*. Art, life.

Chapter 12
Action

September 2, Friday

Dreams of hitchhiking. I could dream all day...

light
inseparable
appearance & emptiness

Inspiring video of Tar Sands Protest at the White House, with Josh Fox, director of *Gasland*, being arrested.

Walk to Walgreen's to buy this new notebook; also get poster-board of day-glo pink for a sign:

COVER
THE
CLIMATE
CRISIS

to hold at Channel 7, Carlisle & Comanche, today from 5 to 6 pm. Home to call Lora & invite her; leave message for Akilah. Write Tina, signed "love & evolution."

Sen. Bernie Sanders on Thom Hartmann: human, all too human. The earth has many beings. Oil leak from BP well in Gulf of Mexico still. I'm thinking NPG: Negative Population Growth is what we need. Now I have the idea to message Shrayas & Amber & to make flyers to pass to motorists at the intersection. (record floods in parts, record drought in parts, record heat everywhere). TX has 16% of US beef cows & record drought. Beef prices to go up. A good time to become a vegetarian, or vegan.

1, Tropical Storm Lee in Gulf; Hurricane Katia in Atlantic. Dow down 269. 9.1% unemployment includes 45,000 Verizon workers on strike.

Center for Biological Diversity calls re toxics, asking for money. Nope; later.

USA Today: Obama decides against tougher ozone standards; Republicans applaud.

R. writes: "do you know of any rinpoche giving 'pointing out instructions' for Dzogchen in the near future?" I write back.

350.org: media coverage includes NYT, Huffpo, CNN, NBC, AP, Reuters & Google News.

China is forcing Tibetan nomads into depressing cities.

Lora says she'll meet me at 5. I make a sign for her.

The flyer:

COVER THE CLIMATE CRISIS

Record droughts in parts of the world, including New Mexico. Record fires. Record floods in other parts of the world. Record heat everywhere.

The corporate media cover major events but never the underlying cause of these records:

the burning of fossil fuels.

The Climate Crisis is caused by:

the burning of fossil fuels.

The climate science is clearer every day:

we must get off of fossil fuels as fast as possible for a livable future.

The corporate media don't want to cover climate science because they are part of the business as usual mind-set that doesn't want change. They are sponsored by Big Oil, Big Coal & Big Natural Gas. They care more about profits than about people & animals.

The economy can transform into using clean energy only if the people pressure the media & other corporations. Clean energy will strengthen the economy. Clean, renewable energy will keep the planet from experiencing runaway climate change.

Recently over a thousand protesters were arrested for peaceful civil disobedience at the White House. They were asking the president to stop the dirty tar sands pipeline from Canada to Texas which would mean "game over" for a stable climate. Among those arrested were climate scientist James Hansen & author Bill McKibben. Did you hear anything about this from the corporate media?

We are asking that the corporate media COVER THE CLIMATE CRISIS.

For more information go to 350.org or climateprogress.org. Or friend Bird Thompson on Facebook. Or join us here at KOAT...

Boy, it's hot. 4:51, in Unitarian parking lot, across from Joe Diaz, the smiling weatherman, & Co.

Lora only good for 49 minutes, then we eat at Whole Foods. She's taking Arabic at UNM & teaching a class in City Planning & Law. We agree to skip weekend & Labor Day & meet again at KOAT on Tuesday.

Marie checks me out for after-dinner chocolate & asks how I liked her CD. I imply "not much" but say I want to hear her sing. I couldn't hear her.

Home to message from Chris. Michael Brown is coming Saturday.

September 3

Wake at 4:20 with dream of stupa sangha (people I don't know) & an upcoming date with a brilliant woman.

Om Ah Hung. Focus on the letters.

On FB, Mona Blaber says she'll join my protest. Lora was right; it wasn't record heat yesterday, just 6 degrees above normal. Chris calls back at 9; I sleep till 11 then.

To Santa Fe. I "coach" Craig in chess for 2 hours. Then to the garden of Jupp. Tomato harvest by Jacobus. Grilled veggies & tofu for dinner. At darkness, Michael Brown & his girlfriend show up. She's 24, beautiful. Her name is Erin. Michael is short, old & loves young girls says Chris. I ask Michael about Rawlins coming to live in his trailer. He says he's not into it, that Steve got the idea. Poor Rawlins will be disappointed but Michael has leukemia & enough on his plate. Erin wants to go dancing. I'd take her out if she was "mine" even though I'd be tired the next day.

Home to all night dreams of her & others. An orgy at the stupa!

September 4

Jealousy? Transform it to joy…

350.org: 1252 arrests total; 618,428 signed petition. Next: Moving Planet, September 24.

Nothing from Tina or Shanny.

Carpool with Scott to Copper Mountain. Carol is in Taos so I lead (thanks David, who can't sing). Tara bliss-emptiness complete with cymbal crashes. Scott knows Karen Fox who might look at my room for rent; he gives me tomatoes. Daniel says alpha lipoic acid is good for neuropathy such as that of Chris Rawlins. Corey's husband has it too.

I ask Marie if she wants to sing with me. She's thrilled. I give her my card again. Her skin is magic; her mind is open. Will she call? Erin had a huge white SUV & drove all the way from Cruces. FB photos of Shannon & Aaron on a beach, in a liquor store.

5:30, New Orleans pumps work to stave off Tropical Storm Lee. 102,000 homes & businesses without power from Irene. Storms interfere with college football opening day.

September 5, Labor Day

I asked OR for a dream of him; dreamed of his new church.

By the lift of my legs, by the sweat of my brow, by the breath of my lungs, by the beat of my heart, by the water of my streams, by the plants of my fields, by the sun of my sky... I haul my body up the Pino Trail for an hour or so...to this spot off the trail a bit where I can do guru yoga. I brought a sandwich of peanut butter & apricot jam. Maybe I should go for the top...

No hikers for a while now; quiet hillside. What year did Walt Whitman die? I think of him as I loaf at my ease, observing the ponderosa. I'm at about 7600 feet; the top is 9200. But I don't have enough water.

Conversations go by. I eat & read.

Go down. Little boy asks his dad, "how come there's a picture rock?"

5, floods in Japan from typhoon, 34 dead. 5:30, tornadoes & floods in US South. TX fire, 500 homes gone in the pines; 63 new fires yesterday. US Postal Service volume down 22% from 5 years ago.

Sue calls. She just finished her jigsaw puzzle. She asks if I'm going back to work in October. I say I'm having doubts. I tell her of my little protest...

September 6

Naked women at stupa. Kids too. I play a new song & another musician likes it.

Tina is moving to Boulder!

NYT: climate change increases cholera outbreaks. New estimate: 8.7 million species on Earth (not including millions of bacteria). Only 1.25 million are known. It would take another 1200 years to describe all of them; a huge number are going extinct. Star may be the oldest (13 billion years).

Poodwaddle.com says world population in 10 years to be 7.576 billion. I say it will be less than now due to climate change. But what do I know? Born to die.

I do phowa practice. "Bless me & others so that just as this life is over we will be reborn in the Land of Great Bliss!"

Nick has burned me a CD, *Speaking in Tongues*! Just what I asked for. We record "The Universe," etc. but I have trouble singing "Falling in Love with the Earth." I'll pay him in October when I can get at my money. Scrimping until then.

I go by Whole Foods but Marie isn't there. I wanted to see if she could come sing Thursday when Nick comes again. "We're in for nasty weather" —Talking Heads, 1983. They've got me dancing instead of lying down. Once at a party (pre-Shanny) I danced to the whole album. "I got a girlfriend with bows in her hair..."

Gas & oil pipelines to China under construction across Burma will earn Burma's military leaders $29 billion over the next 30 years.

47 minutes alone on the corner with my sign till the rain comes. Lora couldn't make it.

Roswell's new record is 109 straight days at 90 degrees or above. Old record was 72 days. Interconnected banks could fall like dominoes.

Lonely Are the Brave with Kirk Douglas. Based on Edward Abbey's *Brave Cowboy*. The Sandias provide an escape route for the foolish cowboy & his horse in this cheesy B-movie. "Life Can Never Cage a Man Like This."

September 7

Wake at 4:40 with the Talking Heads in my tired head. It's Guru Rinpoche day, the 10th day of the new moon.

NRDC on FB gets me to call Obama. It's busy. An hour later it's still busy.

175

Copper Mountain Pureland: imagining being in it makes me happy (& others too I hope). Call Akilah & leave another message. Lora can't make it to the protest so I'm not going today.

RigDzin Dharma is having Amitabha practice on Sunday, 9-11, for love, healing & peace. Maybe I'll go. Om ami dewa hri.

Nine Nobel Peace Laureates urge Obama to Reject Keystone XL (including Desmond Tutu & the Dalai Lama). I make another sign: "Stop the Tar Sands Pipeline."

8 am in Tokyo. Katherine explains the landslides from Typhoon Talas. On the local news there is murder. All illusory, as is my tiredness. 38 degrees Celsius in LA says Saki. That is 100.4 degrees Fahrenheit. Storms Katia, Maria, Nate—unusual convergence says Diane Sawyer. And there is a supernova in M10 galaxy, the Pinwheel. It's 21 million light years away, bright as all the other stars in that galaxy. It was an earth-sized white dwarf…

When I am happy may the merit flow to others…It's cool & breezy; no fans needed today. A car-free day.

September 8

Dream of Rick in a suit, selling annoying toy squirrels that claw at you.

NYT: Gernot Wagner, "Going Green but Getting Nowhere"— "The environmental situation is so dire that even if you tried to become 'no-impact man', you'd have no impact."

Rush to dermatologist. It's beautiful Monica Romero. She looks at my 6 pounds of skin & finds nothing bad except for my lip. She numbs my lip. Waiting to be numb, I listen to Sirius radio pop blend of romance & study the wall charts of skin diagrams. I've worried about my skin for 55 years, always wanting smooth skin like Monica's. She comes back & cuts off the questionable wart for biopsy.

I go to Whole Foods for a bottle of liquid lunch so I don't bite my lip. Marie says she can't sing this afternoon.

I throw a Mo, a Tibetan divination. One die, thrown twice. My question: should I go back to cab-driving? The answer is AH, AH: The Stainless Sky. Equanimity. Giving of fearlessness. Offer to the Wisdom Sutras. I guess that means it doesn't matter, but I'm puzzled.

Flooding from Lee in PA & NY causes evacuation of 100,000 people.

I don't feel so well. Is it the anaesthetic? I call Nick to cancel this afternoon's session. We'll do it tomorrow.

CP: Polling expert: Is Obama's reluctance to mention climate change motivated by a false assumption about public opinion? Europe has 2946 megawatts of offshore wind energy; China, 102; US, 0. Arctic death spiral continues: sea ice volume hits record low for second straight year.

5, KOAT corner. I hold my sign while listening to Obama's jobs speech. Jeff on a bicycle stops; he works for the USGS, takes a class on climate. I give him a flyer. Lora shows up after her Arabic class at 5:40.

Saints at Packers. Dolphins don't form pairs; sex is a group activity. PBS.

September 9

Dream of spaghetti marinara with rich group of people at the cab office.

A gray day. Depressed by lack of media democracy at KOAT.com. Not worth posting on. What did I expect? CP? Channel 7: "Cover-ups You Can Count On."

Nick records. I cheer up even though my voice is undependable. He thinks I'm good. Soup & cornbread at Whole Foods. Klassie & Marie together.

CP: Binghamton NY gets 7.49" of rain. Previous record was 4.68" in one day, last year. The water holding capacity of air increases by about 7% per 1 degree C. warming. Obama gives strong jobs speech, decries "race to the bottom, where we try to offer the…worst pollution standards." David Koch met with Governor Christie before NJ pulled out of successful carbon reduction program.

It's time to go to the corner again. Lora will come. It could be a good hour of mantras & prayers watching the cars go by. But it's rain-shortened again. Home at 5:25. ABC: high alert in NY & DC for 9-11 anniversary. Possible car-bomb threat. Be afraid.

September 10, Saturday

Scattered dreams; another gray day. To the State Fair parking lot in a cold wind. I buy a $10 "Rebuild the Dream" T-shirt & put it on over my fleece. Eric Griego is there, running for Congress. Veterans for Peace float is followed by 60 of us with T-shirts & signs. One of us is a goddess, an ICU nurse with a "Workers of the World Unite" sign. My sign is "Invest in Green Energy." The crowd loves us.

At the end of the parade, an old veteran falls off the trailer & cuts his head. I ride with Dallas to my car; she's kind of cute. Short hair; I wonder if she's gay. Talking Heads home through traffic: "I love every living creature..."

My father Bird would have been 98 this year; grandfather Bird, 144.

CP: Murdoch's NY Post Fabricates Statistic to Vilify Green Jobs. Natural Gas Bombshell: Switching From Coal to Gas Increases Warming for Decades, Has Minimal Benefit Even in 2100 (A Bridge Fuel to Nowhere). Are the Chinese Using Predatory Pricing to Knock America Out of Solar Manufacturing?

Off to the Sierra Club kickball game. Attending: Amber, Shrayas, Christina (cute newcomer from PA, here for UNM grad school in fiction), Paul, Annabeth, Tammy & her little dog Spunky, & Zack. Strenuous fun; I fall down a few times. Nobody cares about the score. Christina lives close to me. She follows me to Whole Foods & we do a little tour, trade phone numbers. She's so sweet; she helped kick coal in PA.

5:30, NBC News is 95% 9-11 coverage. US-centric. Past-centric. Snow in Taos mountains; bear shot in Las Vegas NM. I'm tired & sore.

When to call Christina? Tammy nice too, older. C. says she has cookies & milk every day.

Focus on mantra, then let go. What's there?

September 11

Wake at 4:30.

Breakfast: Christina wants to be friends on FB. I gave her a flyer. Oops! She's in a relationship with Jon Moore. Sun over South Sandia Peak at 7:15. She's just 23 years old!

Yale.edu. Poll re climate change:

12% alarmed
27% concerned
25% cautious
10% disengaged
15% doubtful
10% dismissive

Back to sleep. Wake up tired & sore & lonely.

NFL, meditate, nap. Feel old; ribs sore from falling down.

News sums up post 9-11: 2 million served in Afghanistan & Iraq; 6,123 died; 45,000 injured; cost $6 trillion. Arab Spring this year repudiates bin Laden's philosophy of violence.

Dodge commercial says humans have 3,000 thoughts a day. That's about 3 per minute.

September 12

Orange clouds at sunrise.

#28: "Even hearers & solitary realizers, who accomplish only their own welfare, strive as if putting out a fire on their heads. Seeing this, taking up diligent effort—the source of good qualities—for the sake of all beings is the Bodhisattvas' practice."

I post on Facebook: All this week, Monday-Friday, 5–6 pm, Comanche & Carlisle, Channel 7, KOAT: "Cover the Climate Crisis" protest during rush hour. Join us!

At least 61 Kenyans dead after pipeline explosion. Krugman: euro at risk. Collapse could be a matter of days.

Steve Biko's death in South African prison, 1977 on this date. Let Peter Gabriel sing. "You can blow out a candle, but you can't blow out a fire…"

Full moon day; virtue multiplied…

Tina must be busy. I'm thinking about Florida, the simple way to simplicity. I could just retire there. I'd probably have to move before I die. But renting a room from Jody in Denver might work. Driving a cab would be OK & stay here to see what develops. Phowa retreat in 9 days with OR. Health not good today but will go to Channel 7.

Email from Anne/Rigzin Drolma: we can connect with APR through the 7 line prayer of Guru Rinpoche: "Hung. Northwest Orgyen's border there, on a blooming lotus stem, powers amazing & supreme,

widely known as 'Lotus Born,' with dakinis all around, I do practice as
you did, please send your waves of splendor, guru padme siddhi hung..."

About the Author

Bird Thompson is also a musician, poet & avid chess player. He was born in Pennsylvania & has lived in New Mexico since 1982. He has practiced Tibetan Buddhist meditation for more than four decades.

Bird's original music & videos can be found at www.birdthompson.com.

Made in the USA
Columbia, SC
31 August 2017